Private Worlds

Private Worlds

Growing Up Gay in Post-War Britain

Jeremy Seabrook

PLUTO PRESS

First published 2023 by Pluto Press
New Wing, Somerset House, Strand, London WC2R 1LA
and Pluto Press Inc.
1930 Village Center Circle, 3-834, Las Vegas, NV 89134

www.plutobooks.com

British Library Cataloguing in Publication Data
A catalogue record for this book is available from the British Library

ISBN 978 0 7453 4842 1 Paperback
ISBN 978 0 7453 4844 5 PDF
ISBN 978 0 7453 4843 8 EPUB

This book is printed on paper suitable for recycling and made from fully
managed and sustained forest sources. Logging, pulping and manufacturing
processes are expected to conform to the environmental standards of the
country of origin.

Typeset by Stanford DTP Services, Northampton, England

Simultaneously printed in the United Kingdom and United States of America

Preface

This book marks the sixtieth anniversary of my first published work. In 1963 I began writing for *New Society*, a publication whose purpose was to describe and explain the transition from industrial to post-industrial society. My first article was an account of my mother's family from the late eighteenth century to the 1960s drawn entirely from an oral tradition, where our own history was narrated from memory, without the intervention of genealogists or the plantation economy of family trees.

This became the basis of my first book, *The Unprivileged*, published by Allen Lane in 1967. Since then there have been more than fifty others. These deal with a wide range of subjects, from the sex industry in Thailand; a comparison of child labour between nineteenth-century London and contemporary Dhaka in Bangladesh; and poverty, both in Britain and South Asia; to urbanisation in the global South; victims of 'development'; men who have sex with men in India; refugees in Britain and their flight from tyranny; and the labour movement and the garments industry in Lancashire and Bengal.

I have also collaborated with other authors, notably, Winin Pereira, former atomic scientist in Mumbai, with whom I wrote *Asking the Earth*, an early critique of the spread of Western development to South Asia; Trevor Blackwell, with whom I collaborated on a history of the working class and *The Revolt Against Change*, which argued in favour of a conserving radicalism; Imran Ahmed Siddiqui on India's Muslim ghettoes, Saima Afzal on forced marriage, and of course, Michael O'Neill, with whom I wrote plays for theatre, tv and radio, and who is the subject of this book.

I have also written many articles and books about my home town, Northampton, including *The Everlasting Feast* (Allen Lane, 1974) and *Mother and Son* (Gollancz, 1980). Versions of some of the anecdotes and stories in these publications appear in this book, although none of the material about my relationship with Michael O'Neill has ever been published.

I would like to acknowledge the support in recent years of the late A. Sivanandan, Jenny Bourne and Hazel Waters, and staff at the Institute of Race Relations, editors at *New Internationalist* and *Resurgence*; thanks also to Sugata Srinivasaraju in Karnataka, Iqbal and Brishty Hossain in Dhaka, Ivan and Wisia Ruff, Victor Schonfield, Adele Rijntes, Marcia Saunders, Sonia and Ben Wisner, and especially to my partner, Derek Hooper.

Jeremy Seabrook
London, October 2022

Private Worlds

This is the story of a friendship between me and Michael O'Neill, gay men who grew up in the English provinces while homosexual activity between men was still a crime. Our relationship was inflected by secrecy and fear; and when the prohibition on same-sex relationships was partially lifted in the 1960s, we were already well into adult life. The shadows that had distorted our friendship during adolescence and beyond were never wholly dispelled. The result was an entanglement of dependency and resentment; the rich and satisfying attachment we might have achieved was never realised.

The transformation in attitudes towards sexual orientation came too late for us. Although we lived through the moment of gay liberation, it never really lived through us. Legislation is a blunt instrument, and many people whose sense of self was formed under the taboos Michael and I experienced, remained for a long time with an impaired identity. 'Cultures' are not changed by fiat, but are organic, living entities, which respond in their own time and at their own pace to an always evolving popular sensibility.

The reticences over our sexuality were eventually overcome, and we acknowledged the sad absurdity of such a long concealment; but a bitterness remained, and the relationship never recovered from the damage which the social and moral circumstances of the time had inflicted. This book records the consequences of a relationship distorted by fear and evasion. Some of these still have the power to astonish me; others became clear only as I wrote.

It seems to me essential that, even in the changed conditions in which young LGBTQ+ people now live, we remember a past shadowed by oppression and concealment. It is important for at least two reasons. First, in order that the struggle for the acceptance and tolerance of the present moment should be understood by those who have had no experience of the harshness of the era in which their elders lived; and, second, because there is no social progress and no privilege gained that may not be reversed. We have only to look at how quickly liberal social attitudes of the Weimar Republic were annihilated under Hitler; while the recent controversy of a conservative-dominated Supreme Court in the USA over the *Roe v. Wade* settlement of almost fifty years ago has shown the power of determined reaction to contest the most humane legislation. In the 1980s, the wave of homophobia engendered by AIDS ('the gay plague', as it was called in the popular press) reminds us of the fragility of 'progress'. In any case, almost 28,000 homophobic hate crimes were reported in 2021–22 by the 45 territorial police forces in Britain – no doubt a significant underestimate of the true number. And when we consider the increase of intolerance in populist regimes all over the world, the dangerous lure of nostalgia in India, Russia, Turkey and Brazil, among many others, and observe the re-emergence of a far right thought to have been vanquished in the Western world, we come to understand the fragility of what had been regarded as permanent political improvements.

In spite of this, there has probably never been a better time than the present to be gay in contemporary Britain; although this by no means extends to all alternative sexualities. And it should never be taken for granted. As Thatcher's attempt to turn back the clock in the 1980s after the moment of liberation also confirmed, what has been conceded can always be suspended or taken back. Nothing in human societies is irreversible, and this truth means there is a high risk even when existing tolerance appears at its most unshakeable.

This story is both an elegy for a doomed friendship and a reminder of what always remains, for any minority, a provisional tolerance in need of constant defence. I can, of course, tell only my version of the story; and however unfair this may be to Michael, the thwarted tenderness and the affection we never expressed are still tempered by the laughter we shared and the pleasure we took in each other's company for a quarter of a century. It is presented in memory of Michael and is testimony to a love that was extinguished by quite avoidable socially created shame and denial.

ൟ

Michael was taken into the nursing home in South Norwood on his seventy-ninth birthday. It was a Friday evening, and there was a shortage of staff. When we visited, none of his things had been unpacked. A low-watt bulb shed a muted light over the hospital bed, the pallid armchair and greenish carpet. The chef had made him a birthday cake, which some members of staff brought into the room, three candles shedding a faint flicker over the sombre room. Somewhere a voice was crying out in pain.

Michael was disoriented because of the journey by ambulance from the hospital. He looked round at this new setting for his old life. He did not like it. He wanted to be elsewhere; in fact, anywhere else. He could not walk: his toes were swollen and had been bleeding. A stroke had affected his perception and speech.

It was painful to force some modest birthday cheer. He would not blow out the candles and didn't want any of the cake. We were four friends with him. He was helpless, and we felt there was little we could do.

It was sad to leave him alone; and he was alone, because it was time for the shift changeover of staff. Outside, a thin rain was falling on the berberis and cotoneaster that surrounded the building. He was at least not in the dementia wing. The building was three storeys, with a car park in front and glass doors which had to be opened remotely. We wrote down our initials beside the time of departure. It seemed disloyal to leave him. We told each other he was in the right place, although privately none of us thought it was. Professional care. It was supposed to be for a trial period, but everyone knew he would not go home again.

He raged in the home. Whenever we visited, he would sullenly allow himself to be fed the raspberries that were his favourite fruit; but we understood that was only a truce. When we were not there, he created constant disturbances; as indeed, he had done all his life. But this time there was no one to collude or share in them.

I think I saw him about half a dozen times after that. Early in December, another close friend was admitted to hospital, where he died a few days later. The next two weeks were consumed by that catastrophe. I had planned to see Michael immediately after Christmas.

A call on Boxing Day forestalled it. 'Michael is dying' was the terse message. My partner and I drove down to South London and arrived only a few minutes after he had died. The staff asked if we would like to see him. I said Yes, but it was a mistake. He had clearly died in struggle; his arms and legs were bent inwards. He looked as small and thin as an insect. There was nothing to do. The staff were waiting for the undertaker. A nurse tried to place a pillow beneath his head, but it slipped aside. I kissed him on the forehead; the first time in our life together I had ever touched him with affection.

That seemed to be that. But that is never that, when the relationship has been as long and as intense as my friendship with Michael was. Actually, both words – relationship and friendship – do not really cover the attachment between us.

All profound relationships have the quality of being a *folie à deux*; an intimate departure from reality, an imaginative

4

creation of a world apart; perhaps this is a way of calling forth meaning – the merging of senseless subjectivities.

We all recognise the truth of this in love relationships; the private jokes and use of phrases unintelligible to outsiders. When Proust described the passion between Swann and Odette, making love was referred to as *'faire cattleya'* after the showy orchids which Odette wore on her corsage – he was evoking a level of intimacy intelligible only to the two individuals concerned.

The creation of private worlds is not confined to intensely intimate relationships. Similar bondings occur between conspirators and criminals, where remoteness from reality prompts acts of terror or violence against enemies, real or, perhaps more often, illusory.

Intense friendships, too, may engender a closed circle, in which two – sometimes more – people support each other in eccentric or perverse ideological positions or emotional situations. These sometimes spread, drawing in strangers, so that cults form, attracting the allegiance of people to outrageous or bizarre beliefs.

Something of this occurred in my experience with Michael. It was with him that I first discovered a non-familial affinity when I was eleven. This was seen by my mother and aunts, obsessed as they were with the primacy of kin – 'your own' – as a gesture of betrayal and a neglect of the duties of kinship. But it lasted a lifetime. And it led us to share some strange delusions.

৪০ ୦୪

The first time I saw Michael was in the second year at grammar school; he was telling a group of boys that he had read Gibbon's *Decline and Fall of the Roman Empire* before he was ten. None had, of course, ever heard of that work, but they seemed impressed by his erudition: even in the environment of the grammar school, which fostered a profound incuriosity about the world, feats of intellectual prowess sometimes commanded respect, although they never reached the levels of regard achieved by physical violence or sporting success. Being clever granted a certain immunity from bullying, particularly if the clever ones were willing to do the homework of the strong and dominant.

The second thing I learned about Michael was that it was his ambition to become a member of Parliament for the Labour Party. This assertion defied two conventions; first, in an overwhelming conservative (and Conservative) atmosphere, the voicing of such opinions was both eccentric and subversive and, second, no school child in that place of little learning had ever been heard to give expression to such a fanciful aim in life.

My own ambitions were at this time more diffuse; but that I expected a distinguished future was not in doubt. The problem was that my area of distinction had not yet defined itself. This attracted me to the clarity and precision of Michael's future. I calculated that wherever it might lead, it was bound to be exciting, and that I would be well advised to accompany him there.

The circumstances were disposed to create all the suppressed enmities of a close – and closed – friendship. Neither of us knew that at the time, and it took many years for the antagonisms to appear, although they existed from the beginning. Initially they were concealed by a collusive relationship founded precisely upon a kind of voluntary unknowing about each other, particularly upon the unacknowledged secret of a shared sexual orientation. We had both experienced a characteristically repressive upbringing, not in its Victorian heyday, but at the moment when it was on the point of being overtaken by more benign practice. It had already long deserted the site of its origin, the upper classes, and had filtered, like so much reach-me-down ideology, to the respectable working class, who clung to it tenaciously. It was in the virtue of hard-working towns and puritanical provinces, where people voted Labour and proclaimed solidarity with those like themselves, that such views assumed a tyrannical self-righteousness. This experience lent our (upward) social trajectory a certain poignancy and at the same time a sense that we were betraying those who had encouraged our ambitions.

In any case, repression has many forms; and in spite of living through an age of relaxation, even, some claimed, of 'permissiveness', this had little effect upon our relationship, which froze at the moment of its formation. Only when it thawed in the tepid springtime of its dissolution could we understand the feelings that had been embalmed in the *pietra dura* of its solid ice.

ℰℛ

Although we did not know it, we had both been – I won't say 'victims', because that suggests considered and deliberate actions – of those unfulfilled women, our mothers. It was the social, intellectual and spiritual repression of women that compelled many to seek compensation in an obsessive concern with their children. We became their lives. They identified themselves with us, and we often identified with them, a current of collusion and sympathy, often against tyrannical or indifferent males, many of whom were, in their way, polygamous; being wedded to drink, football or gambling, sometimes to other women; less often to work or trade union activity.

On this unpromising basis, Michael and I constructed a friendship, a rickety structure full of sour laughter and a certain rancour against the world, which had effectively outlawed our sexual orientation (this was the 1950s, a decade characterised by the conservative rigours of conformist affluence). It says a great deal about our instinct for survival and our capacity to overcome severe emotional disabilities; we were surrounded by the compulsions, not only of a form of 'manliness' which celebrated its 'brawn' and its capacity to knock out the teeth of anyone who gave offence, but also by the cases of homosexual depravity revealed weekly by the *News of the World*, which exposed the shame of people like us to public scorn. Our relationship came to depend upon a degree of premature cynicism and a feigned lack of feeling which we spared neither the world nor one another.

If Michael's story was more accessible than mine, this was because of my mother's formidable power in the retention of secrets – even though these did sometimes leak from the impermeable space to which she thought she had consigned them, like a poisonous gas which my brother and I absorbed with our breath until it made us light-headed. The result was that our apprehension of the world was misty and distorted, and even the familiar landscapes of childhood saturated with mystery and puzzlement.

Michael was, in a number of ways, also a war victim; not in an obvious sense – his house was not bombed, he did not have to flee his country, he was not orphaned. But for the first six years of his life, his father was absent, in North Africa and Italy. During that time, he was not only his mother's principal companion but also her reason for living. Their isolation was compounded by their evacuation in 1940 to Northampton, for them a contemptible backwater, whose people were reminiscent of the slow ruminants which formed the basis of the local leather industry. Adelaide hated their suspicious nature, their sly inquisitiveness, as much as she detested the tanneries, the feral breath of the town, exhaled by the factories which filled the streets, clung to the garments of the workers and even insinuated itself into the taste of its bland wholesome food.

ℰᴏ ᴄ℞

They arrived at Castle Station* when Michael was two, where those upon whom evacuees were to be billeted, lined up to inspect the arrivals from the slums of London, whom they regarded with provincial suspicion and distrust. Those who would offer hospitality to the unwelcome guests had a choice. Michael and his mother were passed over by several potential hosts, with comments about needing a good wash or looking as if they had head-lice. In any case, to the mind of our towns-people, all the inhabitants of London were the same, rough, foul-mouthed and assertive. The women were forward, the men fast-talking deceivers. Michael said he and his mother were the last to be chosen and were taken off by a sour-faced woman who told them how much she hated children. She need not have been so concerned, Michael said, because he was already more adult than she was.

Adelaide had all the consolations of widowhood without bereavement, and the enjoyment of motherhood unmarred by an intrusive male presence. With her husband away 'in the war', which became a kind of location – almost, it sometimes seemed to her, a resort – she could devote herself freely to the relationship with her little treasure. It was not as if there were any other diversions. In the bare room they occupied, in the narrow bedroom grate of which smouldered a few greyish coals, there was not even a radio for company; only the outlook onto the street, with its red-brick houses, not quite

---

* The material in the following pages is taken from what Michael and I wrote when we were working on an autobiographical play, *Sharing*, in the early 1970s, with a grant from an Arts Council which was less stringent about its beneficiaries than it has since become.

identical, for they had all been erected by separate speculative builders in the 1870s. Adelaide's only distraction was to
observe the slight differences in style – an ornamental shoe-
scraper, a tympanum with some stained glass, an ornamental
grille around a windowsill, a carved keystone. The bed was
lumpy, and they were fed miserable pieces of gristle, suet
pudding, tripe and watery custard with stewed plums. She
soon found work in a factory canteen, without the supplementary feeding from which, she said, they would both have died
of malnutrition.

She detested Northampton from the start, an emotion which
that puritanical strait-laced town reciprocated. The people
looked at her with disapproval, because she dressed smartly
and carried herself in a way that suggested she knew how to
have a good time. Time, in that grudging town, was not meant
to be good. It was meant to be endured; at best got through.

Adelaide had been raised by foster-parents in a great stone
structure of model dwellings for the labouring classes, called
Little Dorrit Buildings. She had left school at thirteen for
service in the Georgian house of a famous musician. The
mother had renamed her Ada, since she considered the name
Adelaide too pretty for a servant. She did not hold the post for
very long. She was too impertinent for her employers; and in
any case, she had heard of the new industrial estates that were
opening up along the Great West Road, and she soon found
work in a cosmetics factory, where she packed face-powder
into dainty square boxes covered with cellophane. This created
freedoms previously unknown to the former serving classes of
the capital; and it was not long before she was dancing with
soldiers in the West End, doing the foxtrot under the big
crystal ball at the Rialto. There, she met Bill, who was on the
dining cars on the railways, where he picked up fabulous tips
from people like Gracie Fields and Jessie Matthews. That had

been living! And now, here she was, a petitioner for the charity of bovine slow-witted provincials.

Adelaide always took Michael to work, where he was petted and admired by the women. He sat with a story book, or watched as they rolled pastry, a dazzling white blanket which they flung in the air to turn it on the floured board. They peeled potatoes till the skin of their fingers was crinkled and prised the green knots from the long stalks of Brussels sprouts.

He was a sweet and easy child; and she took what she, perhaps, occasionally sensed was too great a delight, in her little man. She made clothes for him out of scraps of material – little dresses, bootees, blouses, leggings. She had never thought of herself as either temporarily or permanently widowed by war; but here she was, consoled by the little boy who was clever and cute, and whose growing intelligence delighted her as she watched it unfurl day by day. She shared everything with him – her thoughts, her secrets and her bed.

She had few excursions. Women did not go alone into pubs in our town until they had reached a certain age. The price for that privilege was to have abandoned any possibility that they might be perceived as sexual beings: they wore hairnets, scarves tied in a knot, shapeless fawn coats, even kept on their pinafore and wore slippers. No man was likely to mistake them for those rare women, 'blondes with a navy-blue parting' or 'whores at a christening', which was how the occasional sex worker in the low taverns in the town centre were known. But the women who had, by their neglected or dowdy appearance, declared that they had done their bottom button up for good, could sit in the snug and tear to pieces the wanton and wayward over a cream stout. That, and the inexhaustible recitation of their illnesses, were the scant recreations of those who survived into old age – which meant the sixties in that era of limited longevity. These women were wardens of an unrelenting Puritanism, vigilant patrols on the lookout, both for sexual irregularities and lapses in the stern duties of kinship.

Adelaide was not of an age or temperament to join what she regarded as a sisterhood of the disappointed. Occasionally she would go to the Social Club, where she met American soldiers on leave, and with whose love of life she felt a powerful affinity. They knew the meaning of fun, a concept still alien to the occupants of our town, and they laughed a lot, showing teeth white as snow and sharp as blades. She took Michael with her, in defiance of a notice that declared the premises closed to minors. He served a dual purpose of seduction and protection against predators.

The soldiers loved him. They picked him up, threw him high into the air, so that he seemed to be flying. They caught him in their strong hands and smiled with their minty breath. When they invited Adelaide to something stronger than a half of shandy, she looked reproachful and said sadly, 'With my husband under the desert sun, wondering if the next bullet has his name on it', and they were chastened by her virtue, and hoped that their own wives and sweethearts were as constant to them as this paragon was to her absent man. It was not, perhaps, that she feared any disturbance to her relationship with her husband; it was that with her son that she wanted to protect.

Michael, it soon appeared, was not only an attractive and clever child, but also showed no aversion to the limelight. He would stand on the table, his little button-over shoes steeped in spilt beer, and the whole club would fall silent as he performed 'On the Good Ship Lollipop', the image, they said, of Shirley Temple without the curls.

The Americans showered him and his mother with small luxuries – candy, gum, fizzy drinks, nylons, which they bought at the base and distributed with a recklessness that evoked the mysterious Atlantis from which they had come.

80 Q&

But like every paradise, this one was also built with eviction in mind. The endless war came to its term, and Michael's father returned. One sunny day in 1945, Michael was fetched from school by his mother, who told him there was a surprise waiting for him. As he entered the kitchen, he saw a khaki back-pack on the floor. There was a scent of tobacco, and a pair of boots lay under the table, suggesting an intrusive presence that regarded the sanctuary as his home also. Michael hated the boots, with their snaking laces coiled menacingly over the lino.

When his father picked him up, he howled. Rage, desperation, grief – everything was spoilt. He recognised it in an instant.

To Adelaide herself, the devotion to her son swiftly appeared in a different light. She was conscious of a sense of shame, as though she had been caught out in an act of infidelity while her husband had been away. She had been indulgent – not only to Michael, but to herself also. There would have to be changes in the domestic arrangements. Michael's feelings may have been clear, but Adelaide herself did not regard the return of the hero with untempered joy. She had found a certain security and contentment with the child, and this she would have to renounce. She had given way to a deceptive complicity in the manless indiscipline of wartime.

She would forfeit her lenient and easy-going involvement and try to address the obscure discontents of William, who came back strangely unsettled by the inexplicable fulfilment he had found in army life. When he spoke of his experience, he did not evoke terror-filled nights, in which every bright light in a starry sky might turn out to be the object that would destroy you, but rather, a time of bonding and friendship, as the men peeled potatoes together, played a harmonica, sang refrains unfit for repetition at home. It seemed he had enjoyed his time in North Africa, and although there had been moments of peril, affection and comradeship had been an apparently more than adequate compensation for the exile from family. Adelaide felt that she was the one who had been missing in action, as she had worked and worried for five long years, while he made his time sound like some kind of vacation. Indeed, when one of his comrades turned up a year later, Adelaide was distinctly unfriendly to the handsome young man with his dark hair and bright green eyes, who said he had come down from Newcastle to try his luck in the South. His wife had gone off with some spiv who made a fortune on the black market, and he wished her good riddance. Adelaide was even more disturbed when her husband suggested she get into the little single bed with Michael, while he shared the marital couch with his mate.

Michael felt keenly the unceremonious withdrawal of his mother's affections, displaced from her suddenly over-tenanted heart. By the age of seven, he had already received perhaps the most powerful lesson of his life in the nature of love; and from this he deduced that even the most profound attachments were fickle, arbitrary and capable of being withdrawn without notice. He later admitted that he hated his father at that time; although much later, they would be reconciled. It emerged that there were many elements of a shared sensibility, not the least of them, perhaps, a homoerotic undertow which would override the jealousy Michael had felt on his father's return.

A year later, another boy was born. This event, after the eviction without notice from his mother's affections – and bed – was to have a profound effect on Michael's future life. First of all, it hardened him against emotional entanglements, and taught him that relationships were essentially instrumental. At the same time, although, of course, scarcely articulated then, he wanted to restore himself to the central personage he had been in his mother's life; although there was no question of any such re-establishment with his mother herself. As a result, he sought to occupy a similar position in the lives of friends. He would deploy all the skills of his early apprenticeship in the performing arts, his charisma and intelligence, to retrieve that role, not within the family, but in what subsequently passed for adult relationships, even if they were all marked by the unfinished emotional business of his brusquely terminated infancy. He would set up geometrical relationships – triangular, quadrilateral, in which people, if not actually fighting over him, were in a competitive struggle for his often distracted attention. He would re-enact the trauma of childhood, seeking each time a different outcome from that which had scarred him; even if he sometimes discovered that infantile glory does not always fit well with relationships between adults.

The relationship with his brother was constrained during Michael's adolescence, although in later life he would become his brother's staunchest ally and support. He grew up to be a passionate activist, a trade unionist who worked for the Royal Mail, a fighter against racism, misogyny and homophobia; a far more practical and convincing radical than Michael or I would ever be, despite the working-class credentials which we did not hesitate to flourish before the border guards on the frontiers of the middle class.

∽ ∾

We were scarcely concerned with our psychological antecedents when we met in Northampton Grammar School, for our attention was firmly directed towards our dilating future. Although anti-intellectual, the school did take some interest in freakish marvels and strange attainments; and there were many remarkable individuals equally in need of friendship and solidarity against the chalk-dust of the classrooms which enveloped learning in perpetual fog, and the mud and pubertal ragging of the rugby-field. Among the eleven-year-olds was a boy who knew where to find wild orchids – early purple, frog- and spider-orchids – in the countryside, another who would become an accomplished composer, who knew by heart the poems of John Clare and another who had already written a novel. My own expertise lay in familiarity with Norse mythology, which I had acquired during a long illness that had resulted in a term's absence from school, and a period of enforced estrangement from book-learning which, at that time, was regarded in our family (as well as more generally) as a recipe for neurasthenia and mental imbalance.

Michael had the reputation of being class-conscious – a state of mind frowned upon by the illiberal academy which provided us with instruction, and which saw itself, a bit like Death, as the great leveller. For having acquired the knowledge and sagacity which it would bestow upon us, we too, however humble our origins, would be in a position to manage the family firm, pursue our own business, become members of the Town Council and, ultimately, be elevated to the aldermanic benches, with, if our charitable works were sufficiently conspicuous, the reward of a memorial brass plaque in the council chamber, the apogee of social achievement in that forlorn provincial settlement.

We were having none of it. As well as his familiarity with the class structure of Britain, Michael also had inklings about the importance of sexuality. He was, according to his teachers, 'precocious'. He would ask at the public library for a copy of the works of Krafft-Ebing, a writer the librarian, although unfamiliar with him, surmised must be smutty, and therefore to be withheld from the clammy grasp of twelve-year-olds. Michael had discovered that psychiatry did not necessarily regard certain forms of sexual deviancy as aberrant pathologies, but as mere inflexions of 'normal' sexuality; an understanding which, he implied, was purely academic, and could have no relation to anyone we knew.

I was quite unaware of the fact that Michael was already an initiate into the mysteries of sex. How could this have happened? My brother and I were caught fast in a dense mesh of kinship, with nine aunts and uncles and their families on our mother's side alone, to whom our every movement was open for inspection. We were under continuous surveillance: neither the bathroom nor the lavatory had a lock, and our activities could be randomly inspected at all times. Michael had escaped this particular form of captivity, since he had no relatives in Northampton outside his immediate family and was therefore free to explore the mysterious hinterland beyond kindred.

It was then a familiar practice for children to stand outside cinemas, where films deemed unsuitable for unaccompanied minors were showing. Children asked willing adults, 'Will you take me in, mister?' Women rarely went to the cinema alone, because the darkness invited unwanted advances (court cases were a staple of newspaper reading, in which the defendant had been observed to change his seat fifteen times during a performance). Men, in a strange reversal of contemporary perception, appeared safer.

It was not long before Michael discovered – to his satisfaction – how little truth there was in this assumption.* His local cinema was the Coliseum, a tiled structure with a greenish dome and round windows wreathed with stone laurel leaves, more funerary monument than place of entertainment. Michael was drawn to the cinema, not only because parents frequently gave their children sixpence or ninepence to go to

---

* In later life, when Michael became ill, we shared secrets we would never have discussed in adolescence, or indeed, for many years afterwards.

the pictures when they wanted them out of the way because of urgent adult business, but because Michael was intrigued by films that concerned relationships between adults. It had been such a relationship that had superseded his privileged status with his mother. What, he wondered, went on between them, that made children an encumbrance? He hoped to find instruction in the opaque, and often mystifying, representation of sex by Hollywood in the 1940s and early 1950s. He must have found what he sought, because he became accomplished in the infiltration of other people's relationships.

One day, when he was in his early teens, a man had taken him into the Coliseum, and had insisted on paying for him. He bought him an ice-cream from the glamorous woman who stood in the spotlight with a tray suspended from her neck. As soon as the lights went down – the film, he remembered was *Meet Me in St Louis* – the hand of the man sought his; not to hold it, as Michael assumed, but to guide it to the secret folds of his trousers, over which he laid a newspaper; and then moved it to and fro until Michael was surprised to feel a sticky secretion between his fingers. He was even more surprised when the man gave him a pound note before leaving the cinema.

Here was something to ponder. Michael was always quick to draw conclusions from experience; and he calculated that since this thing that happened between men and women could also occur between members of the same sex, and since he had been handsomely compensated for his participation in this commerce, it must be something desirable, forbidden and worth money.

Of course none of this was evident in our encounter at school; but it is possible that I was drawn to a knowing quality which he radiated, and which was perhaps a reflection of the metropolitan sharpness inherited from his parents.

What drew us to one another was not our instinctive social radicalism, but our respective – and very different – experience of repression. If Michael had had his spontaneous response to his mother's overwhelming emotions suddenly stifled, when she was induced to feel guilt and shame at the extent to which she had admitted him into the embrace of adult feeling, I was no less crushed, although by a long process of repression rather than by sudden rejection. Michael's early discovery of one of the meanings of sex was far from liberating; and it was formed on an understanding of the futility of emotional entanglements, since these would, as he knew from experience, only lead to expulsion and unhappiness. What mattered to people most was not to be sought in the realm of fanciful and intangible feelings, but in the most basic physical acts.

Michael's knowledge of what he interpreted to be the real meaning of life also induced in him a powerful sense of guilt. He could never be sure that it was not his fault that his mother had expelled him from the scented bower of her love. This left him with a powerful need of someone who would see and judge him as a good person; a role I was only too happy to fulfil, since I was as terrified of my own feelings as I was of my sexuality, both of which were, in any case, in the secure custodial care of my mother, and unlikely to be released on parole at any early date. Michael sought – and may have found – a kind of secular absolution for his sins in my virginal innocence; although, if he did, I knew nothing about it.

ༀ ༃

My mother's adult life had been dominated by remorse; a remorse embittered by the circumstances of the birth of her twins, me and my brother. Her husband, Sid, had syphilis, which had reached the tertiary stage before it was diagnosed, indeed, even before he acknowledged he was sick. This was not the beginning of her shame: she already felt she had been at fault when, soon after their marriage, he had sought sexual satisfaction elsewhere. There had also been several miscarriages; occurrences which he described, with contempt, as her inability to hold his babies; an accusation which placed her firmly in the category of unfit wife and mother, and therefore scarcely in a position to declare herself a victim of deception, or 'infidelity' as it was then known in the divorce courts.

Later, when I asked my mother why she had married him, she spoke as though individuals in marriage – and not only women – were without agency: as though they were merely performing a ritual necessary for the creation of a new generation; and sexual pleasure, if acknowledged in that chill puritanical community, was only a coincidentally fortunate by-product. For her, as for the majority of working-class people, marriage involved roles rather than relationships. A good husband gave his wife enough to provide for the family. He didn't booze or go after other women. He didn't hit her. A good wife fulfilled her duties of childcare and housework. She was always at home when he returned from work and did not contest his opinions. They came together for meals and in the connubial bed, high and hard as a catafalque, in which they performed what both soon came to regard as marital duties. But their real lives lay elsewhere and were separate; his was with work, football, a game of darts, a drink or fishing; while she tended relationships with children, kinsfolk, neighbours, and lived as the wife of a house, which, many women boasted, they kept so spotless you could eat off the floor; a condition not entirely without certain advantages, since some men were known to have 'drunk away' all the furniture.

This view of married life was already becoming archaic when, in 1933, they took a mortgage on a butcher's shop in a gleaming new suburb of Northampton, a crescent of shops which, following a series of warm summers, were built in a Californian style – painted white, with flat roofs suggestive of ranches, Beverly Hills and a longing for a more fulfilling elsewhere.

Sid's family owned a slaughterhouse and butchers' shop in Olney, a small country town about 14 miles from Northampton, which is why they chose to follow a business uncongenial to both of them. My mother was, however, supremely competent, good with customers, efficient and full of energy. He wanted to get rich more quickly than by the slow accumulation from the laborious efforts of a commerce for which he had no taste. He took other work, which his wife dismissed as 'brainwaves' – he started a timber business, with a saw-bench and engine, which soon closed because he had no customers. He kept chickens, and came home with 500 day-old chicks, which all died in their incubator the same night because he forgot to turn down the heating. He finally invested in a truck, to carry loads of bricks, sand or wood between building sites in the Midlands. He also picked up softer cargoes: women he had met in pubs across the region, and from one of whom he presumably contracted the frightening disease with its hissing sibilants, and which, before antibiotics, required years of treatment with injections of arsenic and mercury.

My mother was an intelligent woman who had been required to leave school at fourteen – despite her teacher's pleas – to contribute to the family income, although by that time, with the rest of her siblings working, they were no longer poor. It would have been seen as gratuitous favouritism, contrary to both social practice and justice, to have allowed her to stay at school. She read widely, and was familiar with Dickens, George Eliot (her favourite writer) and Elizabeth Gaskell. In any rational society, her abilities would have been recognised; as it fell out, not only was her education abridged by custom, but most of her considerable energies and skills were subsequently absorbed by the dual urgency of survival and social concealment. She exhibited a considerable gift for both.

By 1938, after the miscarriages, and with further sexual contact with her husband out of the question, she met an engineer working on a building site. The construction was of a 'roadhouse' on the main road out of Northampton, which would serve the estate where we lived. This idea, which accompanied a more widespread use of cars, was for thirsty drivers, not yet instructed in the incompatibility between motorised transport and insobriety. This man, who was both a skilled craftsman – he restored historic buildings as well as working on new ones – and a political radical, supplemented the education she never had. When she died, among her books were anti-fascist and Left Book Club publications, works by George Bernard Shaw (*The Intelligent Woman's Guide to Socialism*), Robert Blatchford and William Morris.

She immediately resolved that he would be the father of the child she wanted. They fascinated each other. He told her he was building the roadhouse to elevate the pleasures of the working man, so that he would be spared the joyless pleasures of drab street-corner pubs. She said to him, 'Don't talk to me about the pleasures of the working man, or I might tell you more than you want to know about the griefs of the working woman.' He admired her spirit and she his erudition. But when she became pregnant within a few months of meeting him, he was appalled. His wife was an invalid. If it came out, it would kill her. She asked him for an example of any woman who died as a result of other women giving birth. He gave her to understand that she could expect nothing from him. She said tartly, and accurately, that she had already quite enough from him, and promised not to ask for money. She rigorously observed this pledge, even when she discovered she was carrying twins.

Uncompromising diplomat and negotiator, with her husband she made a separate agreement. She would continue to look after him until he recovered. He must stay away from the shop – if anyone discovered the truth, the business would be ruined – and he must acknowledge the children as his own. After that, they would divorce. For ten years, all her efforts went into sustaining the appearances of respectable family life. She would empty the pails of disintegrating tissue that came from his mouth and nose, wash her hands in carbolic soap, exchange pleasantries with customers, prepare meals, look after the babies, while he sat morosely in his chair, resentful and powerless – an experience new to him.

Everything he did separated him from the children who were not his. A warning red cotton was tied around his knife, fork and spoon, his cup and plates were never used by anyone else. He slept in the spare room, a damp mildewy chamber forbidden to us, and which we naturally sought out when no one was around. It smelled of rancid masculinity and mould, a source of fear and fascination. For all we knew, this musty exile was the fate of all men. If this was so, I longed to attain it; attracted, perhaps by the mysterious prohibition that surrounded it.

After a few years, unable to stand the confinement, he took to driving his lorry again. His absences became longer. She did not ask him to account for his movements; although later, she thought she should have done so, since she suspected he was breaking the prohibition on sexual incontinence on which the hospital had insisted.

Our biological father also appeared in our lives from time to time, although we had no idea who he was, or why he visited the house – always in Sid's absence. Since he had told her she could expect no help from him, he, too, remained at a distance. Sometimes he looked at us with a fond possessiveness, at which we bridled. We wondered at the stifled emotion which accompanied his visits and at the small gifts of sweets and playthings when it was not even our birthday. There was a suppressed tension in his presence, a yearning melancholy, which, as I now realise, were the only sign he ever gave of thwarted paternity. When my brother was apprenticed to a cabinet-maker, it was he who had found the employer; and when I went to Cambridge, unaccountably lachrymose, he tried to press a ten-pound note into my hand, which I refused, indignant as if I had been offered the proceeds of immoral earnings; which, although in a way he would not understand, I was.

Repressed sexuality, denial and mendacity, as well as an overwhelming expiatory love, hovered over our cowed and stunted childhood. When we were twelve, our mother did indeed divorce her husband, the man we still referred to as 'Daddy'. I have in front of me a thin paper, dated 12 February 1952, with the heading in Gothic lettering: *In the High Court of Justice*. Beneath, it says: Probate, Divorce and Admiralty Division (DIVORCE) at Northampton District Registry. Below that is a list – Petitioner, Respondent and Co-Respondent. My mother is named as the Petitioner, her husband the Respondent. There is no Co-Respondent.

It goes on: 'Referring to the Decree made in this Cause on the 12th day of February 1952, whereby it was decreed that the marriage had and [sic] solemnised on the 2nd day of June 1930, at the Parish Church of S. Edmund Northampton in the County of Northampton between Gladys Annie Seabrook, then Youl (spinster) the Petitioner, and Sydney Robinson Seabrook the Respondent be dissolved by reason that since the celebration thereof the said Respondent had deserted the Petitioner without cause for a period of at least three years immediately preceeding [sic] the presentation of the Petition unless sufficient cause be shown to the Court within six weeks from the making thereof why the said Decree should not be made absolute and no such cause having been shown, it is hereby certified that the said Decree was on the 1st day of April 1952, made final and absolute and that the said Marriage was thereby dissolved.'

Like most official documents, the inflated – and careless – wording tells far less than the whole story. Of course, whole stories rarely see the light of day; but equally seldom do such official records contain as many fictions as this scrap of paper (it measures about 20 cm by 25). It also conceals a depth of misery endured by my mother which few women would now tolerate.

Her anxiety over the proceedings affected her, my brother and me for weeks beforehand. On the day of the court hearing, which she was obliged to attend in person, she left us with her sister. We were taken to a wintry park, where rust had corroded the municipal green paint of the swings, and their metal chains squealed as they chafed the frame. The chill melancholy of separation had found its way through our leather helmets and hand-knitted mittens and we took no pleasure in the deserted playground. We waited restlessly for her to collect us. Our aunt had bought some Bakewell tarts, a small consolation for what she regarded as our semi-orphaned condition.

Divorce was still regarded as scandalous in 1952, and many right-thinking people withdrew their custom from the shop in protest against an infringement of marriage-vows which some of them, no doubt, also wished they had never made. Some men, having learned from the products of Hollywood much about the shady morals of divorcees, made explicit propositions to our mother. They were not encouraged by her response.

§⃝ ℭℛ

We went back to live in the streets, departure from which my mother's family had always prophesied no good would come. They were triumphant. She had got above herself. She should have stayed where she belonged. Divorce, no one had ever heard of such a thing. As for happiness in marriage, well you don't look for perfumes in a pigsty. They might consider poisoning the old sod, using daffodil bulbs instead of onions, as one cousin had done in a failed attempt to do away with a drunken husband. But divorce – everyone knew that was something for people who wore silk dressing-gowns and drank cocktails out of triangular glasses. It was not for people like us. Sexual compatibility had not yet emerged as a criterion for the success of a relationship. A great deal of conversation between women was a shared lament on the ritual assault by their men on Saturday night, when they got a mauling that smelled of beer and stale pub-smoke.

I knew very little about the secret life of our family. My brother and I were aware that something lay in our past, too terrible to be spoken; and the silence my mother maintained over this enormity became the emotional chain by which she tethered us to her. She would sometimes sigh and say, 'Ah, if you only knew!' Irritated, we would ask, 'If we only knew what?' and she would say, 'Never you mind' or, more menacingly, 'You'll know one day.' By now we knew the script. 'When?' 'When you haven't got me.' 'Why? Where are you going?' 'In me bloody grave, that's where, if you don't behave yourselves.' Chastened and submissive, we begged her not to die.

My brother resisted her efforts to control us. His was a cool and practical temperament, and he resented what he regarded as her intrusive trespass on his autonomy. His self was a guarded sanctuary. I, on the other hand, resembled her, and possessed of the same fretful anxiety, I meekly fell in with her project. She gave us to understand that the evil that had befallen the family was so terrible that my brother and I were also implicated; but not quite as she led us to believe, through guilt by association. She implied that there was something so monstrously irregular about us that no one but she could possibly accept, let alone love, us; and the silent admonition was that no good would ever come of any attempt to escape the cruel destiny against which she was the sole protector. Because my twin resisted her, she concentrated all her efforts on attaching him to her. I thought he was the preferred son, as a result of the intensive attention she gave him; he thought I was the favourite because I appeared exempt from her incursions into psychological territory she had already conquered. This mistaken perception set up a hostility between us that was never resolved.

In view of our respective family relationships, the circumstances were favourable for the – sometimes reluctant – complicities of enduring friendship between Michael and me. Michael made himself at home on the trampled earth of my feelings, while I found a kind of kinship, not in the resentful indifference of my twin, but in Michael's pining for his infantile paradise, a site, we were yet to learn, that belonged only to fools.

Beneath the frozen crust of our shared view of the world lay deep unspoken jealousies. I envied Michael his charm and easy manner with people. I wanted to be his equal in understanding the mysterious sexual motives that appeared to dominate all human relationships. I longed to take part in his anxiety-free excursions away from home – he would go hitch-hiking with other friends, fearlessly entering both the cabs of trucks bound for South Wales or Middlesbrough and sleek limousines whose sinister drivers stopped on the A5 for boys of fourteen. It did not occur to me at that time that he might have resented and envied qualities of mine – for although I didn't have Michael's easy address, I was tall, with a certain elegance. I was also the initiator of the work we did together later, and I had the ability to apply myself to serious tasks, while Michael was sometimes exasperated by his own incapacity to resist the temptations of the moment. None of this was ever expressed, and we claimed a complete and harmonious understanding between us.

℅ ℭ

We became inseparable. We sensed that we were among *the last provincials*: the self-contained communities which produced us – with the function of their staple industry inscribed in the fabric of the town and their hierarchical social structure – were on the brink of a transformation. The working class was conscious of its own dignity and, equally, of the humiliation of the poorest beneath them, and the barely respectable who strove to remain just above them. The higher middle class had long retreated into suburbs, sedate and tree-lined, while the gentry remained in country villages and sent its young to be educated for future duties, which might summon them to distant imperial outposts or to the sandstone parsonage, the lawyer's whitewashed villa with its brass knocker or the draughty parsonage with its cedar of Lebanon and broken Georgian fanlight.

In our upward trajectory, we were aware, not of a path already well trodden, but of the novelty of pathways opening up before us: we were like characters in a fairy tale, before whom briars and thorns magically parted, disclosing a vista far from a working life in tanning or shoemaking. The closest our families had come to gentility was with relatives who had been 'in service' with county or business families. For us, the ambition to make our way in the constrained, puritanical counting-houses of the provincial town was none at all. If it was possible for us to look beyond the limits of the hitherto known world, towards the capital, this also depended upon expanding awareness of a society beyond the provincial and, to some degree, on our identification with heroes of the novels we had read and the biographies of working-class folklore of those whose keen intelligence and native wit had been spotted by bosses, employers or landowners, who had taken them up and educated them out of philanthropy or by a heightened sense of social justice.

Our aims were sharpened by the grammar school education designed to prepare us for the society of a local ruling caste. These we repudiated, since we mocked their ways and manners – shiny toecaps, raising of caps to ladies, decorous conduct which forbade eating in the streets or kicking footballs – all enshrined in the sixty-four pages of school rules issued to each entrant to the grammar school. We were arrogantly intolerant of schoolmasters, with their war-wounds, shiny academic gowns dusted with dandruff, tweeds, and linen jackets for the summer term, tarnished silver-gilt trophies for long-past sporting prowess, suburban gardens and sherry-parties to which we were not invited, and, for a surprising number, also suicidal tendencies, for at least three of the seventy teachers in our school took their own lives. A sense of unease pervaded the early re-acculturation to which we were exposed. It was as if those charged with grooming us for a higher station were not fully convinced of its suitability to altered times, nor persuaded that we deserved it, or that we would be grateful for the advantages it was to bestow.

From the beginning my association with Michael was based upon a denial of feeling. It was a curious collusion, not simply a suppression of emotions. We took for granted not only that any display of feeling was sentimentality, but that displays of sentiment of any kind were a form of self-indulgence. We might have been products of the Spartan rigour of the most repressive public school, in view of our cultivation of insensibility to the susceptibilities of others. We saw ourselves as realists, keenly aware of the dishonesty of those who professed love or even affection. Indeed, we were at the very roots of cruelty, for those who suppress their own feelings gain a sense of invulnerability. There was also a strong vein of what would later be more sharply defined as sado-masochism in our friendship; but if anyone had expressed such an idea – they didn't – we would have been appalled.

I can understand how we arrived at this view of human affections, since it developed under the social proscription on same-sex relationships. But I think we both sensed its falsehood; the more so since what I felt for Michael was an addictive attraction to his company and an erotic fascination with his personality – something not far removed from the love which we claimed did not exist. I still don't know what Michael felt about me, but he was never eager to leave me after we had spent time together, even to the extent of walking home with each other, simply to prolong the encounter. We never alluded to our attachment, but instead, turned our gaze upon the lives of others.

And we were pitiless. We set ourselves up as observers and critics of society. This was the mid-1950s, when the old working-class communities were already in a state of decay, dissolving, as they were, in the benign acid of early affluence. Indeed, it was this that had released us – and many others – from having to follow the principal industry of the towns and cities on which they had been founded, and which had given a livelihood to five or six generations; employments which were, in any case, poised to move elsewhere in the world, and would no longer bind the energies of a majority of the young to the constraints of a single occupation.

We did not know that we were the product of these developments; but imagined, like so many other apparently self-made people, that we would rise socially through our superior intelligence, merit or capabilities. We saw the working class as a given, unchanging entity, and had little idea of its perpetually evolving fluidity; unaware that the people we were leaving were not a static frieze fixed in time but were also developing under the same influences that separated us from them. We would define ourselves against what we imagined to be a permanent background; but background it would remain. We maintained, all the while, sympathy with them, but not in such a way that we would have any wish to share a life on council estate, in factory, pub, chapel or any of the institutions associated with those from whom we could not get away quickly enough. But it was evidently good enough for them. We were, in our way, pioneers of the gentrification of radical politics, future middle-class radicals, whose embalmed notion of the working class encouraged a condescending solidarity, which, paradoxically, increased as their lives diverged from ours.

Our relationship was, at least triply delusional. We thought that our rise out of the working class was unique. We were specially endowed with powers of intelligence never before known in that dour provincial town. It was also somehow more 'authentically' working class to avoid any sign of sentiment, perhaps in mimicry of a machismo we did not possess. In our attempt to show the world how tough we were, how like the laconic males ready with their fists and as sparing with words as they were with money and able to hold prodigious quantities of beer, we celebrated our roots in a culture from which we were being borne away on the last train, as it were, before everything changed, naturally, in our limited view, for the worse.

Class was certainly a strong driver in our relationship, but it was class at its most negative and unheroic in our denial of each other's sexual identity. It was a tragedy for working-class culture that its consciousness could not rise above the limitations of labour, however understandable this might have been: work, although often overwhelming, was not the same thing as society, and was always too narrow a base for any collective activity that would transcend capitalism. As a generation narrowly emancipated from industrial servitude, we understood this; and it also contributed to our reluctance to take part in political activity.

There was, however, another reason for the elision of our sexual identity. It was widely believed at the time that homosexuality was a 'deviancy' that solely affected the upper classes. This view gained credibility from a number of high-profile cases, particularly that of Guy Burgess and Donald Mclean, two of the 'Cambridge Five' spies, who disappeared in 1951 and defected to the USSR, having supplied the Soviet government with British intelligence. This had shaken Washington's confidence in the integrity of the British Foreign Office, since homosexuals were seen as susceptible to blackmail by foreign powers. Britain, anxious to placate the US soon found an opportunity to make an example of highly placed sexual miscreants in the case that involved Lord Montagu of Beaulieu in 1953. The peer, a socialite who was at one time rumoured to be a suitor of Princess Margaret, was charged, along with his relative, landowner Michael Pitt-Rivers and *Daily Mail* diplomatic correspondent, Peter Wildeblood, that they had had sexual relationships with two RAF airmen at a party at Lord Montagu's beach hut. The airmen, threatened with jail and dismissal from the RAF if they did not give evidence against the accused, complied, and the three were sentenced; Lord Montagu received a term of 12 months, while the others were given 18 months in prison. This tangle of international politics, class division and ignorance, augmented by the press, and headlines in the newspapers which our parents bought, inspired in Michael and me a kind of fascinated revulsion against posh homosexual traitors, groups from which we were anxious to place ourselves at as great a distance as possible.

This prohibition was strengthened by other examples of upper class sexual delinquency. In 1953 the recently knighted actor Sir John Gielgud was arrested for 'persistently importuning male persons for immoral purposes' by an undercover police provocateur in a public urinal in West London. At Chelsea Magistrates' Court – where he gave his name as

Arthur Gielgud and his occupation as a self-employed clerk –
he was fined £10 for being 'drunk and disorderly'; a leniency
that was accompanied by the condition that he should see his
doctor immediately for medical advice. His identity might
have gone unnoticed but for a reporter on one of the London
papers, and it was widely and luridly reported. Michael and I
also knew that the then Home Secretary, David Maxwell Fyffe,
first Earl of Kilmuir, was resolved to rid Britain of 'the plague
of sodomy' which he had detected to be ravaging the country.
Prosecutions for indecency increased 500-fold during Fyffe's
tenure at the Home Office.

We were fourteen as these events unfolded. We avidly read
the newspapers which informed the world of such appall-
ing delinquencies; and we were terrorised into secrecy by the
reports of what we might expect if we ever disclosed the mysteries we never even shared with each other. No more effective
form of aversion therapy could have been imagined for our
unfolding sexual self-awareness.

℘ ℧

Michael would call for me on the way to school. We walked
through the cemetery and past the private hospital where
celebrities nursed their addictions and breakdowns. Every part
of the topography afforded us some special entertainment. We
read the gravestones, 'Sleeping Where No Shadows Fall' or
'Asleep in God's beautiful Garden', and we expressed a hope
that that celestial patch was better maintained than the municipal cemetery, where rank weeds grew over uncared-for plots;
and if we thought we could measure the grief of the survivors
in the way the graves were tended, we calculated more accurately its cost in the statuary of distress – empty-eyed angels
turning towards heaven, marble slabs with gilded inscriptions,
scrolls and ornaments and Gothic pinnacles, green glass chips

and everlasting flowers under dusty glass. I even located the grave of my grandmother, a small tumulus with a stone jar inscribed 'Mother', with the names of her surviving children. Michael claimed that funerary monuments were the most reliable demonstration of the artistic taste of a nation, and the discoloured stone and mossy growth on those we passed spoke for themselves.

We were also merciless towards some of the patients from the private hospital. A woman with cropped hair we designated a she-male; two women, sisters, who, we imagined – falsely – had been prostitutes, we called Sickness and Diarrhoea. We placed our ears against the red-brick wall that divided the clinic from the road, and imagined we heard the ravings of the locked wards.

A reputation for being 'clever' was easily won in our town. Perhaps it was because of this that we had so little regard for its history. We knew little enough about its importance in the Middle Ages, when Simon de Montfort supported an uprising against Henry III, with the help of university students banished from Oxford who had – briefly – assisted the rebels in the Second Barons' War. At the time Northampton was host to the largest university in Britain. A weakness in the walls of St Andrew's Priory allowed the king's forces to overrun the town and lay waste its streets: Henry wanted to execute the students, but since these were children of nobles, he desisted.

We knew nothing of the life of Anna Palmer, the four-teenth-century anchoress, Lollard and follower of Wycliffe, who lived close to the medieval church of St Peter, and who was brought before the Bishop of Buckingham on fifteen charges of heresy and one of incontinence. She would not answer the charges of heresy but denied incontinence. She was taken to an episcopal prison, after which all trace of her disappears. We had heard no whisper of the activities of Captain Pouch, a tinker called Reynolds from Desborough in Northamptonshire who, in April 1607, instigated riots in the county against the enclosure of common land by the Tresham family. He was known as 'Pouch' because he claimed to have in his purse a substance that would protect all rebels; he believed also that he had the authority of the King of England and of the Lord of Heaven for the uprising. Several thousand people took part. Reynolds was caught, hanged and disembowelled. His purse is said to have contained nothing but a piece of mouldy green cheese.

We knew, of course, that our puritanical town had supported Parliament in the Civil War, but we had not wondered at the demolition of the castle walls at the time of the Restoration, undertaken as punishment for its mistaken allegiance. We were unaware of the discovery of a chalybeate spring, called Vigo well after the victory of 1702, that had raised the idea of Northampton becoming a fashionable watering-place. In 1784 a new wall was laid out from St Thomas of Canterbury's well to Vigo well, planted with trees 'to form an agreeable shelter', fenced to preserve them from the cattle.

Of the preacher Philip Doddridge we had doubtless heard, but we didn't know that his academy was a seminary for dissenting ministers, or that his was an independent mission, the wide appeal of which would unite the highly cultured with the uneducated; a lesson from which we might have profited had we been more conscious of our own heritage. It never occurred to us that the gulf which opened up between ourselves, beneficiaries of higher education, and our families who had enjoyed no such privilege, could already have been a matter of concern in the mid-eighteenth century.

Nor did our sympathies extend to John Clare, whose lament for the passing of agricultural life was reflected in his love of the most intimate details of the same countryside which had been forsaken by our forebears – just as we were to leave the industrial centre which had absorbed and transformed their lives. Clare, the child of agricultural labourers, left school at eleven, and the death in infancy of his twin sister reinforced his sense of sadness at the passing of the life of the countrypeople. We saw the chalk-coloured death-mask of Clare in the local library and, every day on our way to school, glanced at the red-brick walls of the private asylum where he died; but failed to connect the sense of loss that animated him with our own feeling of the caducity of human societies as the industrial past was already engaged on the path to oblivion its agrarian predecessor had taken.

Similarly, the example of Charles Bradlaugh left only faint traces on our sensibility. Bradlaugh was expelled three times for refusing to take the religious oath in the House of Commons and was, in spite of this, repeatedly returned by the electorate of Northampton until the rule was changed: his refusal of the orthodox pieties of the day found a thrilling echo in the minds of the sceptical shoemakers; a sensibility that also influenced our own, although we carried it away with us, unaware of the origin of the spiritual treasure we possessed.

We were so obsessed with our own future that it scarcely occurred to us that we might have any connection or continuity with a dissenting or radical heritage. We had stolen away like thieves, unconsciously bearing away the gifts the community might have bestowed upon us and failing to recognise either the wrong this did to others or the injury our ignorance inflicted upon ourselves.

ଫ ଙ

Michael came home with me after school, and on most evenings stayed to tea. The front room – which the aunt whose house it was still called 'the parlour' – was opened up for us to do our homework. A fire was kindled in the tiled grate which, because it was rarely used, sent clouds of grey smoke back into the room. Michael was scathing about the furniture. He said, 'The whole concept of this room speaks of the 1880s. Honestly, where did they get these ornaments? They're straight out of the Paris Exhibition of 1889' – he indicated the chenille curtain, a squat table with a brass pot and some Dutch vases, the three-piece with its dark floral covers. He picked up a photograph from the mantelpiece. 'Who's this frosty-faced old sod?' He dropped it onto the hearth and it shattered. Aunt Em came in: 'Oh you've dropped Frank's picture.... What a shame.... The frame's all broken. He gave me that, Michael, when he came back from Archangel in 1920. He was on the boats, taking them off, you know, the White Russians, the refugees. He saw some terrible suffering. That picture's been there all our married life, right till the day he died.'

What she didn't tell him was that he had been invalided out of the Navy with terminal TB, and given a year to live. She nursed him with loving commitment so that he lived for more than twenty-five years. On her brief excursions from home – to have a cup of tea with a sister in a neighbouring street, to do a little shopping in the town centre, she was always restless and couldn't wait to go back to the neat little terraced house, and the face of her husband, a pink smudge in the bed behind the lace curtain. Michael, profusely apologetic, took the photograph to get it reframed. He never returned it.

My mother, who was fickle in her favourites, was suddenly insistent that she didn't like Michael. 'I don't want him here every night. There's something about him I don't like.'

'What?'

'He's not doing you any good.'

'Why?'

'Stay away from him.'

'But we're friends.'

'Friends. Boys of your age. I've never heard such rubbish. If it's friends you want, you might try being a bit more friendly to me. There's your brother. Go and play with him.'

'We don't play. We discuss things.'

'Well don't let O'Neill show his face here again.'

He came the next day as usual. She insisted that he was a bad influence, but despite herself, was drawn into the drama he spun around his life. She, who prided herself on her judgement of character, was seduced by his mixture of charm and histrionics. He told us that his parents often quarrelled, and that if he spent so many hours away from home it was because he could not bear to be in their company. His father had attacked his mother with a carving knife. She had shut the door against him and he had broken the windows to get in. It was irresistible and all quite untrue. From the beginning Michael had a powerful sense of theatre, to which prosaic realities were readily subordinated; and this became a major element in our later play-writing.

When we met Michael's parents, they proved to be mild, good-natured people to whom we became very attached. Michael later regretted the false reports he had given of them and showed himself capable of gratitude and generosity towards them. His adolescent drama was about himself: the exclusion from the relationship he once had, and from which he had been innocently cast out. He spent a lifetime seeking to revise and annul this experience; but it was played out among puzzled individuals who had had no part in his betrayal and loss and wondered why he had singled them out for punishments they had certainly never merited in their relationship with him. After his parents died, he continued to act out the same story, living in a *ménage à trois* or *à quatre*, in which he revised the denouement, was not the outcast child, but triumphantly ran off with the human prize. He was like some figure from classical mythology, doomed to repeated punishment

– Sisyphus, Tantalus, Prometheus; and like them, the chastisement was disproportionate to his guilt.

Between us there developed a deeply satisfying inertia. We basked in a destiny foretold (not by our family or teachers; obscurely, it was in the air we breathed, liberated, as we were, from the constraints of leaving school at fifteen, working in manual labour, confined to the provincial town). Michael was, in any case, in exile from the metropolis to which he considered he rightly belonged; mine was a different kind of unbelonging.

What did we talk about those long hours when we sat in the parlour, long after the coals in the grate had turned to cindery ash, the chenille curtain stirred in the draught, and the sound of the last footsteps had died away on the pavement outside? Principally, no doubt, our future, which shimmered before us, beckoning but intimidating. We would leave behind all that we had known, but magnanimously revisit, condescending from the pinnacle of our achievement, to acknowledge those who had raised us, despite their faults, among which we ranked their poor grammar and absence of *savoir vivre* disproportionately highly. We also talked about our teachers, their sense of having given up on life, their limitations and their snobbery, which, because it differed from ours, we castigated with scornful intolerance. We also developed an interest in sociology: the elevation we sensed awaited, gave us, in advance, as it were, a wider access to the world than anyone in our families had ever known.

It was, in fact, the transient hour of the working-class hero. This was not quite the same thing as the 'angry young man', since we saw John Osborne and Kingsley Amis as middle class, whose alienation was quite different from ours. We identified, rather, with characters in the novels of Alan Sillitoe and Stan Barstow – young men, scowling and mutinous, rebellious rather than revolutionary; a role which Michael assumed with enthusiasm. He became an *enfant terrible*, a one-man scourge of anything that savoured of middle-class hypocrisy. Unfortunately for him, this persona lasted all his life, although its moment of salience was brief and it soon became unfashionable, overtaken by other, more vibrant stereotypes. This left him in later years stranded as a splenetic old man, a cultural throwback, rather than the buccaneering hero of his own life.

It did, however, serve him well for quite a long period, since at that time the liberal middle class was assailed by apparently boundless guilt over its own modest advantages. Towards the end of his life, the ghost of the dashing young iconoclast storming the bastions of privilege, remained, a tattered remnant and an object of pity to those who looked after him, as he continued to rage and fume, without realising that the object of his anger was no longer against alterable social arrangements, but against the irreversibilities of existence itself.

In adolescence, Michael and I were always reluctant to part, because there was no conceivable alternative company that appeared more attractive to either of us. Or so it seemed.

Actually it was not quite so. Michael's discovery of sex stood him in good stead as we reached for a sense of adult identity. Michael's success in this endeavour remained well concealed from me. In fact, a recurring memory is of occasions when Michael unaccountably failed to appear when expected; even when we had made a firm arrangement, and he had promised to be at our house by six o'clock without fail. These missed rendezvous were often on Saturday night. I waited in vain for his insistent press on the bell, and listened for his steps. I would sometimes go to the door and scour the street, swept by a chill north-westerly wind, wondering what could have become of him. The first few times he made some apology – his parents had locked him in a cupboard and gone out; he had had to look after his baby brother (who by this time was about eight); his mother had been rushed to the hospital with appendicitis but was discovered only to have swallowed a button while she was sewing. After a time, he ceased to make excuses; and although I was always disappointed, I made a point of never displaying my unhappiness, because of our unspoken pact that sentiments were a childish waste of time and a sign of immaturity.

But I was hurt; a state of feeling of which acknowledgement was prohibited between us. I could not imagine why he did not come. It never occurred to me that he had another life; and it was only many years later that I found out what happened during his absences that left me with such a strange sense of abandonment and emptiness. Since he was the most important figure in my life, my bewilderment and pain at his absences were signs of feeling made the more unavowable by our refusal to concede the existence of any such thing. My mother, aware of my desolation, would say, 'I shouldn't worry about him. He's not worth it.' 'No,' I protested, 'it's not that. I don't care whether he comes or not.' I was puzzled why I should care so much; and if I could find no reason for it, this was because I was looking in the wrong place; and did not dare to search that unvisited organ, my heart.

೮೦ ೦೪

In the 1950s, before the provinces had become the suburbs of globalisation, a distinctively *provincial* way of life remained; the tenor of our town was as different from the insomniac tempo of the metropolis as from the torpor of rural existence. Almost every town and city in Britain produced a single product in the national division of labour; and each clung jealously to its particular occupation, even though the lives of industrial workers converged; so that the experience of the Newcastle collier, the Glaswegian ship-builder, the Lancashire mill operative and the ceramics employee of Stoke-on-Trent had much in common – hard labour, poverty, drink, the subservience of women, the duties of kinship and attachment to place.

This has been swept away, and with it, many of the social types who peopled provincial society, and in whose existence Michael and I found so much mischievous pleasure. Who now remembers the jilted woman, with her lifetime of grief over the mould-stained sheets and motheaten lace of a wilting trousseau; the guileless faith of the chapel-goer with her sense of duty and lisle stockings; the embittered war-wounded man, with his empty trouser-leg sewn up, selling matches or bootlaces on street-corners; the bigamist, permitted by the economic mobility of men to maintain separate families in different cities; the writer of anonymous letters to moral miscreants; the self-taught, who haunted the public library in search of the education they had been denied; the commercial traveller, who brought early wonders of consumerism to the door before the day of television; the stingy boarding-house keeper, who offered hospitality to the travelling stars of shows that lit up the Hippodrome or Alhambra with their saucy sketches and *risqué* jokes; the teacher of elocution, much in demand by civic figures to avoid the linguistic injuries incurred in the arduous sport of social climbing; the woman everyone sent for in sickness and at childbirth, who laid out the dead and even got into bed with the dying, so they should feel less alone?

In spite of the social rigidity of the provinces, every town had some kind of transgressive space; a place apart, where largely forbidden sexual contacts could be consummated. Many of these were in the open air, along canal sides or parkland walks, on derelict land, in areas of woodland. Money rarely changed hands, because this was emphatically not the 'red-light' district, although such a lurid zone did also exist in every sizeable industrial town.

When we were growing up, the sex-trade – although not then known by that name – was confined to two pubs just behind the town centre; many encounters took place in the adjacent Memorial Gardens, where sculptor Frank Dobson's *Woman with Fish* was regularly daubed with red paint and vandalised by those who, however deficient their sense of aesthetics, at least knew what art *wasn't*; and where the weekend's assignations left a litter of beer bottles, cigarette packets and condoms to confront the sparse attendants at divine service in the nearby church on Sunday mornings.

There was another area, set aside, almost 'reserved', for sexual irregularity, perhaps with the connivance of officialdom, where the police maintained a watchful eye on departures from approved morality. This was a stretch of land known as Cow Meadow, where the river came close to the centre of town, and its seasonal overflow inhibited any building. This was not only a cruising area, but also a site where, in the language of the time, 'adultery' could be 'committed' and extra-marital relationships pursued, generally without the knowledge of any of the 'injured parties' – if there were any – in the affair. I don't know how long this territory had been used for such purposes, but I later discovered that it had been familiar to generations before mine.

The flood-plain was a dark fragment of countryside that encroached upon the urban area. This set it apart naturally, as a reminder of rural life, which was – had been for almost all residents of the town – another world, the abandoned site of a pre-industrial past which they, too, had been eager to forget, whether because of the poverty associated with it or the beauty of a landscape they had forsaken. There was also an open-air swimming-pool, a section of river enclosed by a painted wooden fence, which attracted gay men, although that designation was not, of course, recognised at the time. There was something erotic about swimming-pools in towns where men rarely went out without a gabardine raincoat and flat cap, and women wore pinafores and felt hats even indoors. In the thin plywood partitions that divided changing rooms, holes had been gouged, so that it was possible to spy on those in the next cubicle. It was the only place in our town where half-naked bodies were on display, even if burnt bright red by a spell of summer sunshine, unprotected by any preparations to screen them from scorchings that might lead to cancer. I was aware of the park as a garden of earthly terrors; its shadows spoke of the mystery of sexuality, which I feared might subvert my sense of self from within, and which appeared everywhere in the outside world. Sex was the more sombre for being unspeakable: at home, only the grimmest semaphores between my mother and her sisters, facial contortions and rolling eyes, hinted at the presence of something as aberrant as it was repelling. I feared what I might find out, not least about myself, if I ventured into the inviting recesses of the darkened riverside; although I subsequently learned that some of my school friends had already availed themselves of its anonymity to become initiated into sex, while I remained at home, fretting over lists of irregular French verbs and wondering why I was so unhappy.

But Michael was well aware of this dark place, and the excitement of possible encounters. He was knowing as well as vigilant, and he understood that age was on his side. Although proficient in adult relationships, he could always invoke youthful innocence in the event of discovery. Secrecy, however, in the 1950s, that first period of gaudy conservatism, was the first consideration. Anyone caught 'importuning' in a public toilet would have his shame published in the local paper; a declaration photocopied by sharp eyes and archived in an elephantine popular memory. Deception and conceal-ment – even from each other – were part of an understanding that did not need to be spoken between us.

ɞ ɞ

It was not only same-sex relationships that had to be shielded from scrutiny by both the law and public opinion. The most emblematic story of the sad sexual life of that dispirited provincial past was told to me by Alice, an elderly cousin, shortly before she died in the 1980s. The daughter of my mother's oldest sister, she was born in 1910, and was almost the same age as my mother. She never attended school, because Aunt Liza said she was too delicate, and kept her at home, in defiance of threats from the School Board authorities, as both company and servant. Among her duties were taking the beer-jug to the off-licence, fetching the *Sporting Life* paper and running to the bookie's with her mother's bets on the horses.

Alice's only pleasure was the darts team at the local pub. She was a first-rate player, 'as good as any man', as they told her, the highest form of flattery within reach of their inelastic imagination. During away matches, to which the teams travelled by bus, she made a friendship with the first man who had ever taken an interest in her. Her mother said: 'We'll soon see about that.' She found out, through the extraordinary network of gossip and memory that lay, tight as a wire mesh, over the wayward conduct of the people of Northampton, he'd been done for bigamy, an offence widespread then, but long disappeared from the annals of crime. 'He's already had two wives,' she told her daughter, 'what would he want with a lump like you?' Alice was forbidden to meet him, and even her modest outings for darts were cancelled. She never saw him again. In any case, she had got crab-lice from him, which her mother, although no church-goer, triumphantly announced to be the judgement of a heaven, in which, in other circumstances, she was never slow to express her disbelief. Alice came to our house in tears, saying she had never had a life of her own. She was then about fifty.

But that belonged to later life, long after she had reached a pinched adulthood. In her rented house, with its faded lino and moquette armchair in front of a fire, which her mother recklessly fuelled with liberal sprinklings of paraffin, she told me that in 1924, when she was fourteen, she had gone one late afternoon for a walk in the park of shame. This was always deserted in daytime, unlike the municipal respectability of Abington Park, with its band playing marches and waltzes on Sunday afternoons and its bird cages of moulting peacocks and golden cockatiels, designed to mitigate the provincial ennui of the day of rest. The other park was without any attractions whatever, except the occasional fun-fair, when dangerous men with swarthy faces and gold teeth set up dodgems and carousels and tried to seduce teenage girls with candyfloss and promises of a good time. They didn't have much luck.

While Alice was taking her evening walk, dusk fell, and it was already dark before she had reached the ornamental lights that bordered the Bedford Road, when she was violently seized from behind. A man dragged her into the bushes. He put his hand over her mouth, and, as she said to me when she was in her late seventies, 'He done what he had to do, and then left me on the gravel.' Her choice of phrase was significant: she made it sound as if he was following an irresistible male compulsion, and her status as victim was incidental. When she got home, she was also punished by her mother for being out so late.

I asked her, 'Did you know who he was?' She said, 'No.' But she saw him around town for years afterwards. 'He didn't recognise me, but I never forgot him.' I asked why she had never told anyone. 'I thought it was my fault. It *was* my fault. Everybody knew what Becket's Park was. You didn't go down there unless you were looking for trouble. I asked for it and I got it.' Even at fourteen, Alice knew that the park was to be avoided as a place of obscure but seductive impropriety. She blamed herself. When she spoke of it only a few years before her death, she said she had lived her whole life in the shade of this wrongdoing, responsibility for which she had taken upon herself. Three people attended her lonely funeral. A neighbour, my partner and I stood in the gloom of the empty church. We were outnumbered by officiants at the ceremony, as her remains, enclosing their sad secret of violation, were lowered into the ground.

හ ෴

Same-sex relationships also existed in a twilight of pretence between us; Michael and I discussed them as though it were an impersonal issue, like the threat of nuclear warfare or the Suez crisis. It was part of our concern with 'society', and had no direct relevance to our lives. Such irregularities became public only when somebody was pinched by a police raid and his name appeared in the public pillory which was the local paper. Names inscribed on its unforgiving pages would be remembered for generations. Wasn't he done for indecency, people would ask at the mention of the malefactor's name, even twenty years after the offence. They had capacious memories, in which they hoarded scandal, which neither moth nor rust could corrupt.

Being gay was certainly not unknown to the working people of the town, although it was generally referred to obliquely: she's 'like that', or 'He's always been a bit of a Mary-Anne.' Two female town councillors had been known as 'the heavenly twins'. When Miss D. walked along the road in front of private psychiatric hospital where she had been treated for depression, she would hold onto the arm of her Spanish companion, while people narrowed their eyes and sniffed 'Cheese and cheese.' Close to where we lived two men who called themselves brothers were known as the Nancy Browns. When somebody claimed to have known both their families and it was demanded that they account for themselves, they fled, back to London, where they belonged, it was said by satisfied neighbours (who until then had never a bad word to say against them), since everybody in our town knew that London was the proper dwelling-place of depravity and vice; and it was as well that those who practised them should do so under a cloak of anonymity which did not exist in places where people prided themselves on their ability to distinguish right from wrong.

There were ways of providing a decent social burial for being lesbian and gay in that unmerciful time. One of these was to belong to one of the many amateur theatre groups. A mildly Bohemian subculture existed, centred on the Arts Association and drama groups known for productions of avant-garde plays; while for others, the Church covered a multitude of what were regarded at that time, and still are, by certain evangelical groups, as sinful abnormalities. But among the majority of the people, who had more urgent worries than other people's sexual relationships, there was a mixture of condemnation and a tolerant there-but-for-the-grace-of-God indifference. When such things were disclosed, despite their show of righteousness in normal circumstances, people rarely turned on their nearest and dearest and sent them out on the streets, but closed ranks to protect them. A relative of ours was arrested for stealing women's clothing from washing-lines in an industrial suburb of the town. The women of the family gathered in solemn conclave. Bewildered, they tried to understand what could have prompted such inexplicable behaviour. After hours of anxious deliberation, they settled on the explanation that 'he had a kink,' and that it didn't make him a bad person, certainly he should not be rejected by the family. They would stand by him; which they did. He was actually bound over – that is to say, the court issued an order that such behaviour should not be repeated – but the tell-tale paragraph in the paper broadcast his shame to the town.

Whatever may have occurred in the park, or in other rare dark corners of lives that stood blamelessly open to scrutiny, women were expected to maintain a display of virtue and continence in public. My aunt was one day accosted by a man in the churchyard (used by passers-by only as a short cut to the main road). When she told her sister, my mother asked, 'What did you say to him?' 'I told him,' she said with ribald dignity, 'he could piss his tallow where he pissed his beer.'

In fact, attitudes were more inflexible in theory than in practice. When I went to Cambridge in 1957, my uncle took me there in his new Ford car. He stood in the middle of Trinity Great Court and surveyed it with an appraising eye. 'Course,' he said expertly, 'these places are breeding grounds for homobloodysexuality.' (He made of it a word of nine syllables). 'Stands to reason. All these men cooped up together.' My auntie shuddered and said, 'Please God may it never touch us.' I don't know whether I felt greater mortification at the public utterance of their prejudice, or of my own implication in the objects of their disapproval. I thought it might even have been directed at me; but they were innocent – or was it ignorant? – of what to them was an unknown evil.

Other hints suggested that even in that unenlightened time, before the reforms of 1967, all was not well with the orthodox view that everybody was the same, everybody got married, had children, grew up, was given grandchildren so they could die happy, and receive a long list of regrets in the In Memoriam column in the local paper. A neighbour confided to my mother in the 1960s that her husband had never been 'interested in the bedroom side of things'; readily believable, since those austere chambers, with the bare lino, and the china ear of the chamber-pot protruding underneath, freezing cold, and flowers of frost on the inside of the window-panes, were more like sacrificial altars, where the sexuality of women in particular, was ritually slaughtered. In any case, the couple lived alone in the house, and vigilant neighbours had already noticed that at bedtime, lights went on both at the front and the back of the house. The assumption was that 'she'd done her bottom button up for good'.

The poignancy of these observations was viewed by Michael and me with fascinated detachment, which we took for impassive sociological objectivity. This fills me now with sadness and remorse. We learned too late that we should not condescend to, or pity, people, simply because they lived in that doubly distant land, of past and province, where they had to make their own accommodation with society. They laboured under taboos and prohibitions that have decayed in these late, wise times. As we monitored with gleeful amusement the passing of these declining values and customs, we scarcely paused to wonder whether historians of the future might marvel at later social practices, and ask what it meant to live in a society where sex had become like money, something you could never get enough of, a form of abuse a million miles away from the melancholy repressions of times gone by.

80 CB

Much later, when some of the pretence between us had fallen away, Michael explained some of the truancies that had caused me pain and bewilderment I could not express. One night he was drinking in a rough pub in the town centre. The pub was called the Mitre, the episcopal association perhaps mitigating the seedy sinfulness of the drinking-house. Although small, Michael exuded an air of maturity, which enabled him to pass for being much older; and he was rarely refused alcohol from when he was about fourteen. He sat at the bar, next to a scaffolder. Michael opened the conversation, 'How can you drink whisky and beer at the same time?'

'In Glasgow, you know what they do? When they run out of drink and money, they piss in one another's mouth for the alcohol that's left in it.'

'Ugh, that's horrible. I think I'd better go home now.'

The scaffolder restrained him. 'No, don't go. I like you, Spike. I'll tell you what. We'll go for a walk by the canal and I can piss in yours.'

'I'm not gonna do that.'

'Well you can fuck off then.'

Michael was punched in the mouth. There was confusion in the bar. He ran home before the police were called. Next day, he came to the parlour with a swollen face, and told me he had been separating his parents when they were fighting, and his father had hit him with a mis-aimed blow.

If Michael's absences made me fretful and disappointed, they produced in Michael a sense of guilt. While I pretended indifference as to whether he turned up at the appointed time, he persuaded himself that I was beyond the reach of such unwholesome concerns as sex, and he attributed to me an innocence in which he himself could bask, and, perhaps, lessen his own burden of shame. He maintained this feeling for many years; and even as adults, when I shared a flat with him and his boy-friend, he warned friends who came to the flat not to mention sex, because 'Jerry doesn't like that sort of thing.' I would be aware of people looking at me in puzzlement and wonder. I thought this was because I was a curiosity, so bizarre and unattractive that they could meet my gaze only with a kind of pitying sorrow. That was, after all, the 1960s; and although I was, in theory, 'out', it felt more like being a debutante than a proudly gay man.

ℬ ᘓ

We had moved into Palmerston Road in 1955, which my aunt had bought after her husband died and my mother was divorced. It was bigger than the house in West Street where we had lived, which, in any case, was due for demolition. My aunt was deeply upset when her house was declared 'unfit for human habitation'; since this as where she had tended her sick husband for so many years, keeping the small rooms immaculate and placing his food on a tray with a napkin in its ceramic ring and a sprig of jasmine or a pale hellebore.

The new house in the road named after Lord Palmerston soon after he died, had been built in the 1870s on the site of an old orchard, with the result that most houses had two or three gnarled fruit trees in the back garden. We had two pear trees, but the fruits were small and hard and seldom ripened, even though we harvested them and my mother cut them into quarters and preserved them, hard as turnips, in glass jars of syrup. These houses had been occupied by clerical workers in the boot and shoe factories, and for that reason were considered slightly superior to those in the adjacent streets; and although still respectable, the tone of the neighbourhood was already in decline from what it had been in my aunt's understanding. She nevertheless maintained evidence of her rather prim, housewifely skills by fixing a striped canvas curtain to the door each summer, which she brought out towards the end of April and removed in early October. This protected the brushed oak varnish, and avoided its having to be repainted every year.

Michael and I sat in the garden on summer afternoons. We dissected the neighbourhood. Nearby were Ethel Street, Edith Street and Cyril Street, named after the children of the speculative builder who had constructed them, so that we lived in the shadow of funerary monuments which were their bequest to the respectable poor. There was an Upper Thrift Street and a Lower Thrift Street, in which the very provident and the just-provident-enough of the mid-Victorian era had lived. Victoria Road had obviously been named after the monarch: it did indeed contain some larger mansions with steps up to the front door, grilles on the window-sills, and tympanums with sculptured biblical scenes, weathered away to spectral outlines of what they had once represented.

We spent many hours observing and commenting on the people who lived in these streets. Our judgements were harsh and uncharitable; and when I look back on the people we were then, it grieves me that we showed so poor an understanding of those we used to nourish our own – fragile – sense of superiority.

I now see them quite differently, these people who were already disappearing, since profound shifts were taking place in the psyche of those who used to be called 'provincials'. We thought we were leaving them behind; but they, too, were changing, in response to an altered division of labour and a changed social and moral – and urban – landscape. We were living through an extinction of certain social types; a bitter-sweet development, for few miss a declining parochialism, even if people, in the process, sometimes take leave of a sense of place and their own position in it.

In stable communities, life is a series of moral tales, since other people's lives are transparent, and everybody knows *what happened in the end*. They know who finished up penniless, who struck lucky, who was abandoned by their children, who got away with wrongdoing and who got what was coming to them. Physical proximity made it impossible to remain indifferent to the pathos of unrewarded self-abnegation or uncompensated privations; in the provincial industrial towns of Britain tales of injustice circulated in the streets, persistent as the chill West winds.

In the mid-twentieth century, these stories became more poignant because the provincial mentality was in decay; its dissolving certainties turned secrets which had laid waste lives into casual gossip: an illegitimate birth, a shameful illness, mistaken paternity — all swiftly became social history, and ceased to be the tragedies they had been. This devalued lives that had been dedicated to heroic concealment and the maintenance of respectable appearances; victims of an altered sensibility that overturned local pride, identity and codes of duty.

ഋ ൫

The provincial town of two generations ago is more than anachronism. It is a buried civilisation; an archaeological curiosity, preserved only in memory, since it has been smothered by an avalanche of affluence — a social landslide that became sepulchre for the frugal grace and censorious moralism of a way of life overtaken by the incontinent urgencies of consumerism.

The disappeared of provincial life are not simply individuals claimed by time; whole classes have vanished; slipped away unobtrusively, their absence scarcely noticed, the spaces they left quickly occluded. They deserved better than our adolescent intolerance as well as the sleepy indifference of posterity, which always constructs its transient shelters on the graves of forgetting.

Michael and I saw in them figures of fun, and we mocked them from the unstable pinnacle of our youth and its stifled feelings. Later, we felt sorry for the thoughtless cruelty with which we had compiled a dossier of extinct species; and when I re-animate them, I can do so with a compassion which was far from us then, and which makes doubly touching, not only the fact that they have vanished, but also the sensibility with which we looked at them, since we, too, have become archaic, stranded in our turn by a world that has not even noticed our own passing.

They have gone now, women whose principal preoccupation was the minding of other people's business, and who stood assertively outside the labour market, because 'provided for' by their husbands. They were 'houseproud'; an antique virtue which chased the motes of dust in the sunlight before it could settle, scoured, polished and scrubbed, floors you could eat off, and cleaned windows that blazed as though they were the source of the afternoon sun that struck them. They picked compulsively at the fraying social fabric, lamenting changes that could mean only loss, as the last of the retired tradespeople died and those who had gone to 'business' from the once-respectable houses had moved to superior housing they called residences. Where had lived a saddler and a chandler, old gentlemen with white moustaches, gold watches and spats, there came a more slovenly population of factory workers without collar and tie, women with too many babies and young men, clustered under the gas-lamp, velvet collars of their coats turned up, in drainpipe trousers and, like as not, a cosh in their hand. They listened, attentive monitors, for the sound of manners deteriorating; they sniffed the odour of lapsed standards, and kept watch on the subsiding tone of the area.

Insomniac and vigilant, they could judge the state of marital relations at a glance; and sense wrongdoing before it occurred. They could scan early pregnancy with an accuracy that escaped increasingly sophisticated machinery designed for the purpose; and stood in the crowd to witness 'shotgun weddings', correctly forecasting the durability of a marriage to within days of its dissolution. They saw delinquency kindling in the pale blue eyes of snot-nose urchins who blinked at the world from their second-hand prams, already surveying it for opportunities for mischief.

Some puritanical, yet timid, upholders of public morality expressed their concern through the anonymous letter. This quaint practice, once widespread, has now virtually vanished;

displaced no doubt by the identity-free availability of rage expressed online. Letters, without postage stamps, often written in block capitals for emphasis, signed 'a well-wisher' or even 'a friend', fell, gravid with explosive revelations, onto linoleum or wiry doormats. These usually disclosed illicit relationships; sometimes it was abuse, sent in epistolary revenge for some slight or injury. It was a forerunner of much of today's electronic vituperation, which suggests that, as social types vanish, they perhaps reappear in another guise.

A close relative of the wielder of the poison pen was the blackmailer; the rare individual in possession of secrets which people had hoped to carry to the grave. This, too, was one of the disadvantages of a society which had a capacious, even overdeveloped, memory. The silence of the knowing was always a tradeable commodity, and brisk business was done in it. The police warning, the sexual lapse, the moment of dishonesty – all could be drawn out of the rag-bag of remembering to extort a few pounds from the fearful and the ashamed; and there was never any shortage of either in our town.

The bigamist was characteristic of society in transition towards greater mobility. While marriage remained the only licensed premises, as it were, for sexual activity, a growing number of men depended upon travel for their livelihood, as truck drivers, sales representatives or overseers of distant branches of a company. This offered the unscrupulous – always men – an opportunity to set up two or more matrimonial households in different cities, in the reasonable expectation that their wives, sedentary and unused to independent excursions, would never meet. They relied upon the settled nature of the majority to pursue their picaresque adventures.

Occasionally, even in the eventless daily life of our town, a funeral would be disturbed by the arrival of a troupe of tragic strangers, demanding a share in the grief of a family which had imagined itself alone in bereavement. The bigamist (even the word sounds archaic) made great efforts to keep his establishments apart. Economic necessity provided an alibi for men who chafed at monogamy. Bigamy was an appropriately provincial crime, since it hid itself behind the most respectable of facades, marriage; outside of which, sexual adventure was believed to be both doomed (because certain to be found out) or dangerous (since sexually transmitted disease brought to light relationships intended to remain hidden.)

80 03

The provincial town was a place of minute social distinctions, some barely perceptible to the naked eye of an outsider, but an obsession among those bound by custom to a single locality. As the car became more widely available in the 1950s, the mobility it provided perhaps took the edge off the desire to rise socially. It undermined the necessity to do so, since it was easier to go elsewhere and pretend you were something you were not. As long as people were able to observe all your comings and goings, you stayed put, both socially and spatially.

The role of legacies, inheritances and windfalls was significant in social ascent; while the question of people marrying 'up' or 'down', or more critically, 'above' or 'beneath' them, was crucial. Those who enjoyed a precarious prosperity feared 'gold-diggers', while the respectable poor were terrified they might fall into debt, trying to live up to spendthrift or showy in-laws. They were right to be wary. All kinds of incompatibilities were ascribed to misalliances of class, some of them invisible to those not born into the melancholy consciousness of their place in society.

Michael and I used much of what we had observed in this bleak landscape when we started to write plays ten years later.

We had garnered material, in the nick of time, as Victorian ethnographers had done among a vanishing peasantry. We saw ourselves as chroniclers of a working class which we thought permanent, though it was mutating even as we looked on; and much of what we subsequently wrote was already out of date, by-passed by mutations of affluence which we did not really understand. What we took with us to London was already in part historical; and what we conveyed to the – not numerous – audiences for our plays had an aura of the costume drama.

With the effacement of this way of life, long swept away, traces of where people then lived have also gone: parlours with plaster ornaments and plants that survived in no other known ecology, penitential sculleries and freezing outside lavatories, crowded living-rooms with children playing, the continuous sound of radio dance-music, the rustle of the evening paper, the snap of darning thread and the music of cinders dropping through the bars of the black-leaded grate.

The bleak chambers in which people slept have vanished; places where desire was tortured until it died, and marriages remained, indissoluble as a fatal blood-clot. The iron fire grate, unused, suggested also a lack of kindling for human fire. Bedrooms were punitive, hospital tucks and slippery eiderdown, a small square of carpet on which people stood to undress. Even the wallpaper was as unerotic as could be; medallions of pale green leaves on a fawn background, evocative of chaste and faded bowers, while the filament of a bare light bulb shed a faint lustre that scarcely dispelled the shadows.

Only the wardrobe exhaled a breath of mothballs, unworn finery – a fox fur with glazed blue-black eyes, a crepe de chine dress, a shoe-box of pictures of men killed in distant wars, siblings who died in childhood, posing, innocent of their imminent fate, with ribboned ringlets and sailor suits against a table and potted palm. When I think of it now, my sweet

Aunt Em each morning emptying the chamber-pots into a pale enamel bucket, which she then carried to the outdoor lavatory, I feel a sense of shame and sadness that I could ever have thought of allowing this woman, who had suffered the great loss of her husband, to wait on me. In spite of having been, as we imagined, 'liberated' from the working class – as though this had been some kind of prison-camp from which we had by a miracle been released – we also bore away with us not a few of its deepest misogynistic prejudices, as well as our own version of intolerance.

In the bedroom windows of some houses in the 1950s began to appear the plywood back of a vanity unit, a blank triptych of mirrors, in which younger women could contemplate their face and figure from hundreds of angles; contrivances regarded by their older sisters as objects of unnecessary luxury; on the tables before them were set jars of paint and vials which diffused a mist of scent when an attached bladder was squeezed – the whole suggestive of a future still prohibited – in which sexual interest might extend beyond the birth of children.

Giving birth was often put forward as the reason for women's declining interest in sex; or perhaps this was part of a competitive struggle between men and women to deflect blame for a loss of sexual excitement onto one another. In male company, men would say you don't look on the mantelpiece when you poke the fire; while the women would commiserate with each other and wonder how a bit of gristle between men's legs could cause so much sorrow in the world.

Marriages were part of a wider web of relationships, not solely private deals between individuals. People 'married into' one another's family and successful integration depended upon the observance of obligations and duties. They expected to live by a code of behaviour, and rarely assailed one another in search of a 'happiness' to which they thought themselves entitled. Couples entered marriage fatalistically, expecting to be separated by death, not by arrangement. It led to extreme unhappiness for some; but stoical resignation was the fate of a majority; and who, among the fretful and searching of our time, is to censure them for the lack of choices which were never theirs?

§) ⚬Ʒ

In the 1950s, before divorce became commonplace, marital separation remained a shameful admission of defeat, especially for women. The transgressions of men were viewed more indulgently. Nothing showed so clearly the gulf between generations in the 1960s as attitudes to divorce. Younger women whose marriage broke down often found their biggest problem was dealing with the tragedy their mothers made of it. 'Knots tied with the tongue,' said the old women bitterly, 'cannot be untied with the teeth.' Divorce tore up the old provincial morality, which was founded upon the primordial importance of 'your own' against the alien world of 'other people' or 'outsiders'. The structure of belonging itself, it seemed, was being demolished, like the houses in streets where three or four generations had lived and died; and their resistance was vehement.

My mother made a torment of my brother's separation from his first wife, even though any other course would have been destructive to both. She would hold up her ring-finger and say dramatically, 'There's no happiness to be found outside the wedding ring'; even though she had found only misery within its tightening circumference, as its gold bit more deeply into her flesh. As a pioneer of divorce, after the pact with her syphilitic husband had lapsed, she ought, perhaps, to have been more tolerant of failed marriages. She wasn't. She became more strident in defence of an institution that brought her only desolation and grief.

By the 1960s, the portals of the heart, like doors to the rows of houses, no longer stood open to the free comings and goings of those related by blood, but were double-locked against intruders, among whom even close kin were now to be found. In big families, there had always been quarrels and fallings-out; ganging up, alliances, temporary favouritisms and permanent affinities. One minute, they would be thick as thieves, living in each other's pockets, as they said; the next at each other's throats, going at it like cat and dog – the set phrases they used suggested the disputes were passing and not serious. They served as safety valve for the enduring duties of flesh and blood, confidantes to whom they could unburden themselves, and confess their lack of fulfilment or exasperation with those to whom they were tethered. Once they had done so, they would depart, if not happy, at least reconciled to a fate that could have been worse; and there was no want of examples in the community to show them their relative good fortune: the woman who 'put her head in the gas oven', the mother whose son drowned swimming in the river one summer afternoon, the man who had interfered with children on the allotment. A dense mesh of relations who could be trusted was not a small consolation.

ಕಾ ಅ

Strangely, the one exception to our ridicule were the elderly. Perhaps it was their vulnerability which reflected to us the fragility of the structure we had created for ourselves. Michael and I watched the passing of a characteristic English figure, the spinster; but we excluded her from our catalogue of social exhibits. This now archaic term for an unmarried woman derives from the idea that it was women's work to spin, in preparation for their marriage. 'Spinsters' were prominent among the declining congregations of many churches and chapels. If the word is suggestive of blighted lives, this is because many were the premarital relicts of marriages unconsummated, since their men had died in war; and unused trousseaux were hoarded in bedrooms, linen stained with mould, cutlery tarnished by time and ornaments dimmed by dust. Our neighbour, always respectfully addressed as 'Miss Wood', kept into her eighties everything in preparation for the ceremony that never took place, since her fiancé had died in the last month of the war. One day, she took my mother and me into the sombre chamber in which all she had gathered for married life had been stored for half a century. Little by little, acknowledging that none of it would be employed for the purpose intended, she gave my mother wartime soap that failed to lather, lengths of lace that disintegrated when washed.

The room with its virginal double bed was an emporium from the end of the First World War. There was a jug and crystal glasses, a tea-service, each cup cracked inside with age, but still ornamented with garlands of pink roses. Saucepans, kettles and casseroles lay next to unfolded linen, tea-towels that fell apart as they were opened up, sheets fragrant with an ancient hint of viburnum or sweet violet. There were brass candlesticks, a scentless *potpourri*, even some medicines – Dr Collis Brown, Widow Welch's pills and throat-lozenges in a rusty tin.

Miss Wood was a fervent chapel-goer. Such a definition connoted plainness, temperance and enjoyment of pathetically simple pleasures like chapel teas, choir concerts, Sunday-school treats and outings by coach to Symond's Yat Rock. Chapel-goers were stranded, a little like the beleaguered chapels themselves, gaunt buildings encircled by the forbidding moat of an inner ring road. The people who attended these depleted places of worship, were dowdy, ageing and curiously innocent of the modern world. It was as if preoccupation with their immortal soul had prevented them from hearing the good news that had superseded stories of posthumous salvation – that it is the here-and-now that truly matters, and the life to come has been downgraded into a pretty story to soothe infants, and teach them a wavering right from an uncertain wrong. The chapel congregation, elderly innocence and bony morality, continued to believe in the goodness of people, even when the truly instructed had recognised that selfishness and greed were the real motors of human endeavour, and had adapted their conduct to these late revelations of our true nature.

We would choose a different denomination as an object of scrutiny each Sunday; where guileless ministers welcomed as 'new blood' and directed their, alas, not very powerful sermons to us, as though welcoming the repentant back into the fold. Although we could not share the enthusiasms of the scant congregation, we were aware of the poignancy of the situation, the sparseness of everything – attendance, refreshments, thinning hair in cavernous buildings in which damp and mildew left the shapes of mysterious continents on blank walls, and a little sunlight filtered through some crooked leaded lights and illuminated the dust to which all knew they must – and soon, because they were elderly – return.

We were sometimes silenced by the faith they expressed through a sense of duty and service to others; unrewarded care-givers to infirm parents, bringers of broth and kind words to the afflicted, unpaid runners of errands for the housebound and bedridden. It was they who tended the wandering mind and helped gather the scattered wits, cleaned up the incontinent and looked into the eyes of the dying. They stayed awhile each day with the invalid, observing a neighbourliness which stopped short of intimacy; and offered themselves spontaneously on the doorstep or at the threshold of the sick room – the opposite of the minders of other people's business, for they were minders of other people.

℘ ℘

Apart from these rare moments of sympathy, Michael and I wandered through the lives of such people like anthropologists; the very embodiment of a colonial superiority, which we deplored in its more visible form, but which we also embodied in our own sense of apartness from, and position above, those with whom we had grown up.

I have often wondered why we were less politically committed than we certainly ought, in retrospect, to have been. There were a number of circumstances which at that time contributed to our sense of political disengagement. One was the assumption of the inevitability of progress, which had had the wisdom to elevate us, and, in the form of the welfare state, would surely look after those we were destined to abandon. Fear of the exposure of our sexual orientation was also a factor. Our attachment to an idea of the working class also involved tribute to an idea of male supremacy which was not widely contested in the 1950s, and which we would not have dared to call into question, since that would certainly have opened us up to – accusations? suspicions? – of what we also saw as aberrant behaviour. What should have been a source of assertive identity remained a shadowy vulnerability at that time; and this was something we did not care to display.

In the meantime, we trampled the threadbare fabric of the provincial heritage, imagining that we were overcoming obstacles which had already been removed from our path, both by loving parents and by the – then – humane agencies of the state, which made our social levitation appear as effortless (and as impersonal) as an assumption into heaven.

Among the most poignant of our social observations was the passing of the self-taught workman and woman, which we registered without regret. Plentiful in the 1940s and 1950s, consequence of a triage of the poor that kept them from all but elementary education well into the twentieth century, if their struggle for learning was heroic, it often left them with a grudge and a sense of inferiority. This was not entirely allayed by hours of patient study, in library, night school, trade union classes or those of the Workers' Educational Association. Their communities were the richer for their efforts; a steady stream of callers at their house would ask for help in letter-writing, interpreting the opaque instructions of officialdom or intercession with the forbidding institutions of the state.

If Michael and I reserved for such people an especial mockery, this was because we knew that we would have been like them if we had been born only a generation earlier. We looked at them as symbols of a fate we had only narrowly escaped. If they appeared remote from us, this was because the education we had received – and despised – gave us access to a world they had had to discover for themselves, in libraries and at meetings in dusty ill-lit rooms after a hard day's factory work. They could be churlish, and expressed contempt for gossip. Truculent, principled and uncompromising; they embodied the best and worst of the local sensibility: if they were self-righteous and pig-headed, they had a strong sense of justice, were unimpressed by fine words or snobbery. After 1945 self-improvement came to appear unnecessary, when the state was eager to undercut any do-it-yourself instruction. They looked upon teenagers in the early 1950s as alien beings and, aggrieved, complained that when *they* had been lads and girls, they vowed to leave the world a better place than they had found it. Moved by idealism and social hope not yet forlorn, they had laboured, so that not even the weakest and most feckless would be left behind by the advances which they foresaw.

In their front rooms stood glass-fronted bookcases of the classics, a set of Dickens, and encyclopaedias falling apart with use, from which they had gained much knowledge that was useful and a great deal more that was not. They assumed the role of teacher, preacher and social worker; and if they were viewed as eccentric when things were going well, as soon as trouble came, everyone knew where to turn. They forgot meals, failed to turn up for meetings, for their mind was in the ruins of Persepolis or in William Morris's futuristic landscapes of socialism, from which ugliness and misery would be banished. They inhabited other worlds, yet remained anchored in this one, since they struggled daily against the strife and pain of people destined for a lifetime of work, to which their energy, youth and eventually, health and hope would be sacrificed.

8○ ○3

The insularity of the provincial town could be gauged by its reaction to those who came to settle there from outside. The Londoners who, like Michael and his family had come during the Second World War, continued to be looked on as aliens, years after the end of the war. Even my childish experience of them spoke of unfamiliar characteristics, slovenly charm and precocious sexuality: one boy delighted us in the gorse-fields, by making a long piece of grass disappear into his urinary tract; another taught us the shameful delights of masturbation among the unerotic shit and feathers of a hen-house. Soon after the war, 'displaced persons' appeared; no more outlandish idea could be conceived than these personages mislaid by time, who had no home to go to, since they were stateless. A girl called Ingrid taught me Estonian when I was seven. We sat on a sunny doorstep, and the only word I can remember now is *aken*, meaning window.

Economic migrants were sighted only in the late 1950s, and must have occasioned the same astonishment to the protected of the provinces as they had to those adventurers and buccaneers who, centuries before, had set foot on the territory of others. We had been brought up to sing in Sunday school, 'Over the sea, there are little brown children, Fathers and mothers and babies dear, No one has told them the Lord Jesus loves them, No one has told them that he is near'; a song I learned when I was eight, and which offered reassurance to the people that the good news would speed swiftly over the water to let them know they were to enjoy all the benefits of posthumous salvation. That some of them might one day appear in our parish, with different notions of salvation in mind had never entered the head of those homely people so firmly settled in Midland clay that they had taken root there like the ubiquitous crab-apple and birches of the landscape. One elderly aunt, whose idea of geography was, in any case, confused, said that when she stepped out into Victoria Road, she no longer knew whether she was living in England or Zululand. If our sympathies were not with the outraged parochials of Victoria Road, perhaps we should have spared them a little more understanding than they were ever shown by political leaders or those to whom their slender education had been, nominally, entrusted.

If we had been more astute we would have recognised what was actually happening before our eyes, and we might have understood the significance of our detachment from those we loved. The communities in which we had been born were being impoverished by our removal from them. It was at their expense that our personal ambitions were to be realised; and we were pioneers of a desertion, as it were, which would soon become a mass exodus of able and competent young people who left working-class towns and cities for higher education and an irreversible sundering from those who had cared for them. This was a loss which the people had never chosen. But then, they had never been consulted on anything that had happened to them since the beginning of the industrial era – or indeed, at any time before it. No one ever chose to be part of the great upheaval that had transformed a wasting peasantry into industrial workers; and once it was established, no one was asked if they wanted to see the demolition of the manufacturing base to which they had long accommodated themselves. To adapt to unchosen change had always been their fate; and over time a deep reservoir of – perhaps – subconscious resentment and anger had been perpetually replenished. This deepening estrangement from a growing sense of powerlessness – despite electoral 'choices' which often seemed to make no difference – really burst forth only in the referendum on leaving the European Union; and it revealed to ruling elites a long-term alienation they had never before taken seriously. That Michael and I contributed in our small way to these great shifts in sensibility never occurred to us as we sought to make our way – and it was *our* way – in a world we thought was simply bestowing upon us the privileges we thought we merited.

ഔ ൫

One of our teachers at the grammar school, to which we went in 1950, had fled Austria after the Anschluss in 1938. He was highly conspicuous, even flamboyant. When he taught us German in the early 1950s, he was already in his forties. Thick-set, with black hair, he wore double-breasted suits and spectacles prescribed in pre-war Vienna. He wore an air of disorientation, emphasised by his pronounced accent, his manner of pompous courtesy and formality. His very presence, articulate and intellectual, set him apart from the townspeople. He also exuded an aura of unhappiness, and was subject to the anti-Semitism which persisted in spite of the war against Hitler. Even other teachers spoke of him slightingly, showed an amused tolerance of his exuberant and *continental* manners; continental manners which, few of his colleagues guessed, was already sending all remaining members of his family to Theresienstadt, and thence to Auschwitz.

My first encounter with him was when, sitting on the bus from school, my arm was wrenched violently so that I was compelled to stand up; and a furious face thrust itself into mine, saying, 'Can you not see that there are ladies standing while you remain seated?' Terrified, I vacated the seat, and a perfectly fit young woman sank gratefully into place, sighing with admiration at such old-world gallantry. I was terrified by this assault; dreading the example that would be made of me, a brutish eleven-year-old who left *ladies* standing, when it was well known that the delicacy of their constitution exacted a sedentary position whenever possible. This episode, and my fear of the repercussions of such an enormity, made me ill; and I managed to avoid school for three weeks after that, and avoided Mr Buchwalter until he became my sixth-form German teacher. He tried to teach us about the *Aufklärung*, which made it sound like a weather forecast; and we preferred to remain with our heads in the provincial clouds.

I left the school without regret, and assumed my contact with this unfortunate man would cease. It didn't. I later returned as a teacher, and the man who had appeared as ogre became a colleague. He showed the over-eager friendliness of the lonely; and we did have interests in common – not only in exile and the recent history of Europe, but also in the theatre and literature.

He was living in a flat on a recently completed estate on the outskirts of town. At that time, council accommodation was still regarded as a fitting habitation for the middle class, and not a social dumping-ground. One day, he invited me to tea. We stood on the balcony overlooking a patch of sunny green. He told me one of his sixth-form pupils, an accomplished painter, had, during the summer holidays, brought his easel and paints and set up on the grass in full view of the teacher's house. Mr Buchwalter was disturbed and excited by the boy's persistence. It was obvious he wanted friendship. Mr Buchwalter decided not to speak to the boy or even to recognise his presence; although he frequently looked out from behind the curtains that floated on the summer breeze; and observed the boy wistfully looking up at his window. 'He made it so clear,' the elderly man said sadly, 'that he wanted to talk, who knows. I didn't acknowledge him. He never came back. He left school and I never did know what became of him.'

Mr Buchwalter was one of three members of staff at our grammar school who took his own life; which suggests an unhappiness, not only of exile but also of an isolation scarcely to be borne in that forcing-house of respectability, with its casual anti-Semitism and deep incuriosity about the world it was supposed to be preparing us for.

If Michael and I were scathing about the class with which we were familiar, we detested even more the instruments employed to groom us in a snobbery in which we, alas, required little instruction, although those who inspired *our* sense of exclusiveness came from further afield than the mildewed propriety of rows of bungalows with hydrangeas, carefully arranged crazy paving and chiming door-bells. We had been beguiled by the mysteriously diffuse call of a prosperous and liberal middle class, of whose existence we had heard, and with whose sensibility we imagined our own might be more in tune than with the dour, sour mentality of the leather-workers we knew too well. Although we had little direct experience of this class, we heard its voice continuously through the 'wireless'; and I learned to speak without a local accent under the tutelage of BBC announcers.

80 03

As time passed, other transients became familiar; theatricals, who stayed in the town's few and comfortless boarding-houses, leaving behind a disturbing savour of tawdry glamour and loose morals. Some of these Michael also got to know, no doubt in the same clandestine way that made odd strangers greet him in the town centre as we wandered through the market square on Saturday mornings – house-painters in dirty overalls, timid solicitor's clerks, elderly men with a touch of eyeshadow. 'Who are they?' I would ask anxiously. 'Just somebody I happen to know,' was his evasive reply. I tried to dismiss the unlikely connection, but something about the familiarity, indeed, if I had recognised it, intimacy, fretted at my somnolent consciousness.

The theatre people who appeared in troupes performing musical comedies like Edward German's *Merrie England* or the thriller, *Dial M For Murder* were not exactly stars. They shared lodgings with a known – and distrusted – type, the commercial traveller, who, at that time, rivalled them in glamour. These sales personnel were always male; bringers of messages from the future. Some, more showy, drove cars, but the less well paid arrived at the station on Monday mornings, suitcases full of samples of merchandise. They wore lovat-green suits, gabardine raincoats, trilby hats and brogues; objects of growing interest, since it was mainly through them that new items of consumption first reached us. Colonists of consumerism, their presence was faintly subversive; because they were introducing destabilising products which might undermine the placid tempo of daily life and lessen the labour of women. As ambassadors of the time to come, they were seen as a threat to the moral order, both economically and sexually. They had accents from elsewhere, and it was known that those who travelled door-to-door were also on the *qui-vive*, looking for sexual adventure, since it was known they had had ravenous erotic appetites.

Since men, in that frugal community, were as parsimonious with words as with money, they rarely articulated relationships of affection. Despite this, relationships did exist, which went beyond the known obligations of kinship, neighbourliness and work-place. Men sometimes displayed a certain tenderness within their rough-and-ready daily lives, although words that might have borne the emotions that flowed between them – preferences or attachments – were seldom uttered. Self-deprecating banter or gross insults were the usual forms in which soft feelings shyly concealed themselves.

৪০ ଓଃ

Eddie never married. He regularly took his neighbour's son, Terry, then fourteen or fifteen, birdwatching, fishing or swimming. This boy's father was dead; and Eddie's single state drew them together in an affinity of absence. Eddie was an intelligent shoe operative, who had been a champion swimmer in his youth. Laconic, with a slow sense of humour, he smoked a pipe, an attribute associated with thinking deeply. Terry was slow to reach puberty and was ashamed of his small stature. He had regular features and wore an expression of constant anxiety at what the world might do to him. He spoke with a stammer, another impediment to direct avowal of friendship. Eddie sometimes said that his Mam was his only sweetheart. He was not derided for it.

They would go off in the early morning, fishing rods, nets and bait over their shoulder, towards the river's edge. They sat behind a windbreak of a piece of tarpaulin, long hours among the reeds and bulrushes, watching dragonflies skim over the water and listening to the sigh of dry sedge on the bank. 'There goes Eddie with Terry,' people would say approvingly, when they saw them together. No one suggested there might be anything improper in the relationship.

They caught tench, bream or perch. River-fish were rarely eaten, since they were judged rather tasteless. Eddie's mother sometimes said her son was a bigger kid than his young friend: he would forget his tin of live maggots in the living room, and by morning, they had hatched into a cloud of iridescent blow-flies. Eddie and Terry swam in the still unpolluted river, changing into their bathing-trunks behind clumps of willow or alders.

They probably spoke little. An easy companionability required nothing to be stated. Such a friendship today, if not impossible, would be more rigorously scrutinised, and would certainly arouse suspicion. If no one doubted the genuineness of their attachment, this was almost certainly because there was nothing suspect in it. For one thing, sexuality was more deeply embedded in social institutions than it was to become, and had not yet emerged to dominate all human attractions; and in the cool shadow of silence, it would have been difficult to find anything 'unhealthy' in such a relationship. If the older man took an erotic delight in the presence of his companion, nothing was ever said; and if the boy found comfort in the protective shelter of the man's friendship, this was within the order of things, in which elders taught a new generation what to expect from the vicissitudes of life. We patronise those of the past for their ignorance; and the people we have become are perhaps less enlightened than we like to believe. As we have come to understand, progress is not always inscribed in the lateness of the date on the calendar.

Today Eddie might be labelled paedophile; and Michael and I did not spare them our mockery. Yet the image of the man and boy remains, the modest pleasure of being together, remembrance of an openness no longer available; a measure of losses which our lives have sustained, even among the multitude of undeniable and well-advertised advantages.

℘ ℂℛ

The 'corner shop' is now kept chiefly by Turks or Bangladeshis. Many such places in the immediate post-war period were not on the corner of streets at all, but had been converted from the room of a house. These sold general goods or greengrocery, but occasionally had a more specialised function – Ray Gosling's grandmother kept a flower-shop in what scandalised neighbours thought ought to have remained a 'parlour', but because it was close to the cemetery, it seemed too good an opportunity to be able to remind those who had gone to visit their dead but had forgotten the floral tribute they intended. In other former front rooms, there would be a hairdresser or a children's wear store, where winsome 1930s china dolls modelled school uniforms.

These shops were chaotic and crowded, and the people who looked after them – often women widowed by war – were rarely much better off than their customers, far from the stereotype of the avaricious shopkeeper who sold inferior produce and counted greasy sixpences in a metal cash-box. Some barely survived. A narrow wooden counter divided the room, and the window was filled with a jumble of cheap goods – dolly mixtures and bags of fizzy sherbet, liquorice wood, jelly babies and Radiance toffees, Woodbines, Gold Flake, bottles of fizzy Corona. The interior was dingy, the counter worn from the passage of goods and money across it. Cards of kirby-grips, mouse-traps, buttons, shoelaces, ribbons, buckles, India rubbers, combs, pencils, cotton reels, pen knives, batteries for torches, would be lifted down from nails in the wall with a long hooked pole. Dusty stationery – notebooks, paper, cash-books, together with bottles of ink and sealing-wax were kept in brass-handled drawers that drooped from their cavity in the wall. Indigestion remedies were much in demand to counter excessive carbohydrates in suet pudding, bread and potatoes. Hessian sacks stood on the customers' side of the counter – items that did not risk being stolen – rice (for puddings), flour, dried peas. Bundles of sticks for lighting fires were bound up with a twist of wire, and some shops sold bags of coal or coke.

These were places where monetary exchanges took place, but the trade in gossip, rumour and reputation made up an even greater volume of commerce. If these were convenience stores – a term then unknown – part of that facility lay in the ease with which you could get to know other people's business. The women shopkeepers were consummate actors, and hid their opinions more carefully than their money. This was the site of 'women's talk'; conducted in the language of women, another tongue – inflections, vocabulary, subject-matter – which differed from the functional intercourse of men; and although men had custody of opinions on affairs beyond the streets, they knew little of the currents of feeling that ran through the community, both the dark flow of prejudice and also an indulgent acceptance of human frailties. If men were masters of machinery, sport and political opinion, women knew about relationships; and their conversations showed a familiarity with the human heart, its flutterings and captivities, its hardening and skipped beats, its swelling with pity, its exaltations and sorrows.

A relative of ours had such a shop; accommodating and generous, she knew everything about the people who frequented it, and plenty about those who didn't. She was a big woman, with a wide smile and warts on her face, and she wore a length of hessian around her waist to protect her against the earth which still clung to potatoes, carrots and turnips, still innocent of industrial washing they would presently undergo to make them fit for the shelves of supermarkets. She was a woman in whom people instinctively confided. She didn't fear death, sickness or wrongdoing, as long as people acknowledged remorse. Fierce moralists, yet lenient to weakness, critical but not censorious, these women, too, have gone, since there are scarcely any secrets to keep or relationships to conceal. The confessional pain they absorbed has been professionally channelled to advisers and counsellors and other officially appointed custodians of other people's sorrows; and the women became as redundant as the town's boot and shoe workers, whose labour was no longer required. If their passing is to be regretted, it is not because the need for their healing counsel has gone, but because while they lived, their work was unacknowledged, except, perhaps, by the grateful hearts of the long dead. When I think of them now, it is with a yearning of the spirit, and if we did not appreciate their humanity, this is because we had too readily abandoned our own in expressing disdain for those who have left far more tangible examples of their wisdom and kindness than either of us have done.

ॐ ॐ

The teacher of elocution lived in an avenue lined with scented lime trees. In her youth, she had acted with a repertory company, and later set herself up as a kind of linguistic orthopaedic surgeon to the deformed vowel-sounds of our town, which had its own distinctive – and unfashionable – accent. Although, according to the weathered board outside, she taught both elocution and deportment, there was no great demand for the latter. People visited her, almost clandestinely, as private students, the object of their study being to cultivate social airs which would not disgrace them as they rose in the world. Many pupils were the wives of local officials, councillors and shopkeepers, whose social elevation had outstripped their ability to express it through the spoken word. Much instruction involved learning where and when to drop or to articulate aspirates, and the rounding of vowels; disabilities which prevented them from speaking with the necessary authority to servants and small tradespeople and those whose lowly status called for an imperiousness of manner they lacked.

These social transformations even then appeared faintly comic to many people, and Michael and I exulted in it. We decided to investigate her service from closer quarters. Even in the 1950s, there was something a little grotesque in the caution with which aspirants to the middle class expressed themselves – echoes of this remained in the careful diction of Margaret Thatcher who, even in her moments of greatest hauteur, always sounded as though she feared some indelicate provincialism might leap involuntarily from her mouth. This was sad, because she was herself a forerunner of the new aristocracy of the market, the triumph of celebrity and money, which has such self-confidence that it no longer needs to mimic the manners of those formerly placed above it. This is sometimes referred to as 'the decay of deference'; although deference was never more intense than today: no longer excited by ancient qualities of caste or breeding, it saves its awe for the sheer weight of the wealth of the world, and the millions available to footballers, pop stars and media personalities who have risen through the mysterious levitation of the market.

The elocution teacher never made a fortune out of her clients, but there was a steady stream of little girls who had to be made fit for private schools, and a number of adults who wanted to 'get on in society'; a term which, in that prosaic town, had nothing to do with balls given by the duchesse de Guermantes or coming-out parties for the daughters of the gentry, but access to Alderman Finch's new year's party, civic balls and receptions given for minor members of the royal family.

Michael and I knocked on her door one day and confessed to her our problem. We were hoping to go to university, where no members of our families had ever gone before; but we were at a bit of a loss as to how to behave and conduct ourselves among those more fortunate than we were, who had learned to express themselves with grace and eloquence. She was enchanted by our enthusiasm. She told me that my English was almost flawless, only a few vowels – such as the short *u* in 'bus' or that elongated *a* in bath required correction; but that Michael was hampered by a significant London accent which would require attention. We never returned for a second lesson.

ॐ ॐ

Not all our excursions were so intense. We both had a strong sense of place, nourished largely by our distaste for the town, which, apart from the market square and the seventeenth-century church of All Saints, we said had been ruined by Victorian philistinism. We contrasted the urban grimness with the surrounding countryside, the proximity of which had always been one of the great compensations for living in many of the shabby industrial towns of Britain.

At different times of the year, we would go into the countryside, recognise and name wild flowers, trees, and birds, and estimate the date of construction of houses in the villages; reconstructing in imagination the world of those who had lived there.

One September, we walked through the fields and re-populated them with the farm labourers who would have thronged them two hundred years earlier – the barefoot children with wooden rattles, scaring the rooks and crows from the growing crops; the milk frozen in the churn in winter; women and children gleaning in the fields after harvest; the unwed mother and her children scandalising the village by 'lying on the parish'; the pauper apprentices being killed by their masters, so that they could get a new one with a five-pound premium. On that autumn afternoon we made for the deserted village of Faxton, driven by a fascination with settlements which lose their reason for existence: a foreshadowing of the fate of provincial towns and cities whose economic purpose was also fast vanishing, as the industries on which their prosperity had been built were closing down – and an echo of the villages that had fallen into neglect in consequence of the departure of the young and vigorous for the 'new' manufacturing districts of Victorian England.

By mid-September the trees had changed from the vivid colour of early summer to a sombre blackish green, although the slanting sunlight shone on the stubble of cut corn and illuminated the dry stalks like a field of glass shards. Hedgerows flamed with orange rose-hips and crimson haws crowned with black; the drupelets of blackberry and small chandeliers of heavy purple elderberries. By late afternoon, half the field was in shadow, and the ice-cream cumulus reflected silver in the pale sun. Wild flowers had become sparse – knapweed and thistle a few purple cockades among grey thistledown released by the breeze; and the spiny husks of horse-chestnut broken to release their shiny brown fruit. The hearts and bells of convolvulus trailed through the hedges, a celebratory remnant of summer, and the creamy stars of travellers' joy trailed across brambles on which a few tremulous white flowers lingered.

We left the town boundary along the road bordered by pine-trees, treading on the dry pale grasses on the verge, until we came to the church of Brixworth, one of the most complete Saxon structures in Britain. It had been founded in the eighth century, and partly rebuilt in the tenth, with fragments of Roman brick, probably from Leicester. The stone, reflecting the light from coppery afternoon clouds, transformed the structure into a vessel that had travelled through the impenetrable element of time; its survival, relatively unscathed, is a marvel. In the churchyard, the same names recurred on the headstones; people rooted like the ivy-grown trunks of ancient beech and oak, their overgrown graves largely effaced by orange and grey lichen. More readable were the delicate engraving on early nineteenth-century stones, which give way to Gothicised memorials, sacred to the memory of Samuel and Temperance Turner, who also lost a 14-year-old son in the 1850s: testimony to centuries of abridged and unfulfilled lives, and a reproach to the unreflecting longevity of posterity.

We walked on to Lamport, naming as many of the wild flowers and trees as we still knew, having been taught by parents unwilling to lose all contact with their country past. In some fields the stubble was burning, and smoke rose up in dense grey plumes which dispersed in a transparent haze. The medieval church at Lamport had been extended grandly in the eighteenth century to the glory of the Isham family, descendants of a sixteenth-century wool merchant, particularly Sir Justinian, whose marble bust dominates an interior commemorating his tour of Italy. An old lady was tending the flowers. She took an enamel jug to the tap outside, and arranged a display of early chrysanthemums and asters. Surprised and nervous to see visitors, particularly young men, she was reassured by our politeness, and tentatively asked us to worship with her on Sunday, as though this were a personal invitation.

Faxton lay over two miles of cart track and then fields. The landscape was illuminated by pools of light from the thickening cloud sheet and the earth cracked from three weeks without rain. We sat on some bales of straw in the late afternoon silence. Faxton was a medieval village, probably of Norse origin, and was mentioned in the Domesday Book in 1080. Its decline may have started with enclosures and the replacement of arable farming by sheep. The story is told of this village, as of many others, that a rich London family seeking to avoid the plague in the seventeenth century came to this remote place, but were already infected and caused the death of many inhabitants, even though records show no decline in households before and after the plague. It lost population in the nineteenth century, and the last inhabitants departed in the 1950s. There was a small stone pillar where the altar of the parish church stood. A single wall of a ruined stone cottage was the only structure, although earthworks suggested the more ample settlement; and two red-brick cottages were being restored. The vestigial dwelling showed the trace of a fireplace, green-washed walls, and evoked the deal table, wooden benches and straw mattresses of a comfortless past. Acrid-smelling nettles grew in what was the single downstairs room; and a weasel rested in a pile of stones.

We took a cart track towards the village of Old. People were blackberrying with tins and paper bags saturated with purple juice. As we waited for the bus to Northampton, we asked an old man if there was a shop in the village. 'Well there is, but he's on holiday.' 'We've been to Faxton.' 'I used to go there a lot. Not now. I'm eighty-one. Can't get there. The old lady in the stone house was the last to go. She went to Walgrave before the war. She only died twelve years ago. Things are changing. Not for the better. No matter what government's in, the unions are always on top. They rule the country.' His wife came out of the cottage to join him. She told us she was eighty-five. Her hair was white and her cheeks a network of red veins. 'I went out to service when I was eleven. The Ishams were a lovely family. They looked after us. The quality don't live here any more. But you had to obey. I learned discipline. There's none of that now, they don't listen to anybody. I had to do as I was told, otherwise I was out. I was born in this village. He comes from Lincoln.' 'I drove all kinds of locomotives,' he said, 'and her father was also a railwayman.' She went on, 'I've seen a lot of trouble in my life. I had two brothers killed in the First War, and two others died soon after.

We've three children, all married, with their own families, thank God. A lot of young people leave. There's nothing here.' She invited us in for a glass of orangeade. The gardens of the cottages were communal, with a late nineteenth-century pump. The old people could no longer cultivate them, so they were overgrown with mint, oregano, lavender, sunflowers and brambles. Inside, the table was covered with a chenille cloth, large framed pictures hung forwards from the wall, some sunflowers stood in a jug on the windowsill. The old couple said they could no longer get into town to do their shopping and their life in the village was shrunken.

We took the bus into town. A cool wind was blowing through the open window. A girl in the front seat screamed because a wasp had flown past her. 'Won't hurt you if you let it alone.' She screamed again and ran downstairs. 'Damn silly wench, scared of a wasp,' said a woman to her husband.

80 03

If the lives of the people of the provinces were narrow, their feelings ran deep, and the light by which they lived was scarcely dimmer than that of our own late wisdom. Apparently permanent figures in an industrial landscape, they were ephemeral beings to be swept away by new brooms of money and mobility. No doubt, globalisation also has its own provinces – places, perhaps, orphaned of wealth and still beyond the reach of the ubiquitous global media gaze. No doubt too, we, universal metropolitans of a future which we assumed belonged to us, have also, in our turn, been stranded by time, although in different ways from those formed by local provincialisms. No society or culture can stand permanently, and without intense powers of adaptation, it will succumb even faster. We had no idea, either that all that Northampton represented to us, would vanish so swiftly, and even less did it occur to us that the quickening tempo of technological change would quickly consign us, too, with our faith in welfare, public services and an NHS devoted to caring for all, to the same social oblivion that awaited them

It seemed then that the whole town existed principally for our entertainment; and we enjoyed the spectacle, as perhaps only extreme youth, allied to a certain nimbleness of wit and repressed feeling, can achieve. We went to meetings of the Psychic Society, where rows of elderly women clutched mementos of their dead relatives, in the hope that they would receive the message that death is not the end. The mediums were usually sharp-eyed women dressed in slightly Bohemian clothes and a great deal of jewellery, and were familiar with the kind of people who attended their séances of hope. They looked at Michael and me warily, for they guessed we were interlopers bent on sport with emotions that were not to be trifled with. They would begin with some familiar name, 'I've got an Annie ... or a Danny ...' and someone would say, 'Yes, that was my mother'; and from the beyond they would receive advice or exhortations of extraordinary banality or vagueness. 'She says "Don't put all your eggs into one basket" ...' or, 'He says there are other pebbles on the beach.' The recipients of this intelligence would smile or weep, recognising the wisdom of the departed, and expressing their gratitude to them.

Michael and I tried to smother our laughter, not always successfully. Occasionally we were asked to leave, the medium telling us that we were radiating negativity. Once Michael called out, 'I can see some ectoplasm, it looks like fungus,' and we clattered out of the Carnegie Hall, our footsteps echoing on the stone flags, our laughter reverberating through the building. Feeling somewhat ashamed afterwards, we said we wondered why, if there was life after death, people would come back with such trivial information. 'You'd think they would say something about what it was like wherever they were – something about the décor of paradise or the architecture of heaven.' If you really had experience of the afterlife, why would you come back to remind Aunt Win of the old horsehair sofa in the parlour or the Krugerrand made into a silver ashtray by Great Uncle Joe?

$\wp \quad \wp$

A second great source of less than innocent fun was the Arts Association; a self-conscious group eager to give the lie to the perception that Northampton was 'a cultural desert'. These were earnest and well-meaning people, who certainly did not merit the lofty contempt with which we treated them. We would wait for a talk that looked promising – 'Whither the Novel?' Or 'Verse Drama Today'. The Arts Association met in the council chamber of the seventeenth-century County Hall, a magnificent building, from which we imagined agitators being sentenced to transportation, rioters and rick-burners destined to hang, felons sent hence on a hurdle to a place of execution.

Such grisly antecedents did not disturb those assembled in a semi-circle at desks around a walnut rostrum. The dim lighting gave it a somewhat ceremonial air. We were greeted by anxious women, whom we referred to as nomads in the cultural Sahara. We gleefully listened in, as they said how refreshing it was to see new blood – a greeting that we had become used to in our systematic gate-crashing of institutions dying of old age.

'We're hoping to do *Huis Clos* in April. Do you think it's too advanced for Northampton?'

'In what way dear?'

'Well, it does deal with very delicate subject.'

'What, hell?'

'No dear, Sapphics.'

'Yes but they're all dead, aren't they, so doesn't that make them harmless?'

One night the guest speaker was to be our English teacher, Mr Pickering; the closest the grammar school ever came to a star. His youthful enthusiasm, energy and the faint scent of patchouli that emanated from his well-dressed person was both exciting and disturbing. We thought he would probably shock Northampton's avant-garde, which was as backward as everything else in that slow, unexcitable place. He was to talk on 'The Modern Novel'.

He began histrionically. 'Yes. The novel. We all have one inside us. Like a gall bladder. Let us hope it stays there. In the days when I used to send grubby manuscripts to Victor Gollancz, I was unaware that the novel had already become an archaic form, particularly the modern novel. There is only one English novel in the twentieth century which is worth the time of day. I re-read it annually, at Christmas-time. I take down from my shelf, not Huxley, certainly not Lawrence or Virginia Woolf. I settle down and open the first page; and Joe Oakroyd, Miss Trant and Inigo Jolliphant are all waiting for me, changeless, timeless. Yes, I'm off on my yearly jaunt with *The Good Companions*.'

They were shocked. A few timid questions, 'What about the Proustian vision, Mr Pickering?' He answered grandly, 'Myopic in the extreme. What he needed was treatment, not for his neurasthenia – that was merely self-indulgence – but for his novel-writing, which was a form of mental instability.'

In the sixth form, a friend of ours, defiantly and prematurely open about being gay, met Mr Pickering one weekend in a gay bar in Soho. Embarrassed, he told him he was gathering colour for his next novel. What colour is that, our friend asked, 'pale lilac or baby pink?'

℘ ℃

We went to the New Theatre in the town's main thoroughfare, just before it closed in the mid-fifties. It was by that time a sadly reduced site of spectacles that had once included touring opera and ballet companies, and had descended to showing saucy revues with titles like *My Bare Lady, Yes We Have No Pyjamas* and *Nudes of the World*. It advertised its attraction: 'Meet stars without bras in our bars.' We would queue for the gallery. The theatre was cold, cavernous and empty. While the Lord Chamberlain – the then official censor – forbade nudes to move, Phyllis Dixey avoided this prohibition by standing on a revolving piano. She was charged with, I believe, public indecency by Northampton Watch Committee – a local sub-committee of the council, set up to oversee morality in places of entertainment.

As well as the artistry of women with names like Peaches Page, a comedian would head the bill; someone formerly well known on the halls, but now reduced in late middle age. They told jokes which might once have had people rolling in the aisles, although not within living memory. 'Did you hear about my wedding night? The woman I married, she was a lovely woman. We go into the hotel, honeymoons suite. I say to her "Are you ready for bed love?" She says "Almost, darlin'." To my surprise she takes off her wig. Then she takes out her teeth. She undresses and takes off her falsies. Then she takes out her glass eye and her deaf aid. Not only her titties, but her bum-cheeks are foam rubber as well. She gets into bed, and calls "I'm ready, my love." So I walks over to the dressing table, unscrews my plonker, slaps it on the dressing table and says "Now bloody well beat that."'

A lone cackle from the audience, high and desolate; somewhere in the audience a baby started to cry. We yelled 'Rubbish' and ran down the steps, as the doors reverberated behind us in an echoing clash of metal. I remember after these demonstrations of disapproval I often felt curiously sad. It was not so much the desecration of theatre that touched me, as the sense that people who had built a successful career should have descended so far as to include Northampton on their itinerary of failure.

The theatre was demolished in 1958, and replaced by the first supermarket. This was opened by Sabrina, a TV personality famous for the girth of her bust. The streets were thronged with people, and traffic came to a standstill. A different kind of popular entertainment had already overtaken the theatre.

The demolition of the New Theatre saddened me for other reasons than the loss of 'live' (actually moribund) performances in our town. As children, we had eagerly looked forward to the visit to the pantomime each Christmas. The excitement of this coloured the weeks before the actual event. As soon as I knew what that season's pantomime was to be, I would badger my mother to make sure they booked well in advance. Many of the aunts and uncles came with us – there would be a whole row filled with family members. The smell of oranges and chocolate pervaded the stalls; and as soon as the Safety Curtain was lifted, a fringe of gold was illuminated from below, the orchestra tuned up, and we were about to enter a world where gender-roles would no longer apply. This was, for me, the unspeakably thrilling aspect of the experience. The man-disguised-as-woman, the 'dame', I found unnerving, reminiscent of back-garden conversations between old women, which savoured too much of the familiar and everyday. But the principal boy – a woman dressed as a handsome prince – made my heart flutter; for I wanted to recognise myself in this appealing androgynous disguise. It expressed something prohibited but far more real than the distribution of roles in real life. I was unmoved by the principal girl, and entertained no fantasies about carrying her off: it was the false-boy who exercised the real fascination, and taught me much about a self which, at that time, remained sleeping, but which would stir into a life of intense yearning within a few years; and was already touched by the suggestive promptings of that apparently innocent family outing to the pantomime. I thought, even then, how little adults understand of the effects of ostensibly harmless entertainments on the fragile being of children; and how horrified they would have been, if I had granted them access to an inner life, which remained firmly locked against any trespass they had no intention of making. Afterwards I would go to the mirror in my mother's bedroom, cover my head with her stockings, so that they resembled hanks of hair, and take a smudge of colour from her rarely used plastic cylinder of lipstick. I looked at myself and wondered, for the first time, at the arbitrary nature of the ways in which gender was expected to be indicated.

Only once I made a modest public attempt at cross-dressing, intended only for fun, despite the – for me – serious consequences that ensued. In the lower sixth, at the end of summer term, the school lowered the tone of the social events it was prepared to entertain by holding a fete and fair. I allowed myself (offered myself?) as a female Hollywood star to bring the show to a close. I was to be interviewed by a very correct sixth former, a very sweet boy who had formerly been at public school, but had been forced through family illness to throw himself upon the mercies of state education. (I had been told by the form-master to treat him with special care, because of the social descent he had suffered; indeed it all sounded like a terrible accident, particularly to those of us who were destined for dramatic upward mobility.) I dressed in a green satin frock, with a blond wig and big hat, and pretended to flirt with the interviewer. I then sang, 'Got along without you before I met you, gonna get along with ya now', in mimicry of a US duo called Patience and Prudence. This performance was very popular; until some boys passing by jostled me roughly and sneered, 'Some kind of pouf are you?' This came as a shocking revelation; partly because of its truth, but also because I had not recognised it until it was illuminated by these ill-wishers. Appalled, I rushed to take off the offending articles of dress and to return to my image of schoolboy innocence. I observed Michael's absence, and it dimly occurred to me that he was afraid of guilt by association. As I was morosely pushing the tell-tale garments into a duffel-bag, another boy appeared, one I recognised to be on the edge of the sporty set. I awaited his insult. He sat down on the wall outside the school and said, 'I think you looked very nice.' He paused. He then said, 'I haven't got a girlfriend. Would you like to come to my house?' I feigned outrage and walked home.

ɛɔ ᴄʁ

After that I retreated into an avid studiousness, hoping that my intellect would efface all traces of things which, I was well aware, were not only socially inadmissible but, equally, liable to get you arrested if you tried to do anything about it. Michael did not mention the afternoon's performance; but a few days later, he said, 'You were very convincing you know. A bit too convincing. If I were you, I should be worried about it.' This last remark drove me even further away from any inclination I might have entertained about a future as drag queen – a concept I had still never heard of, but with which Michael was already mysteriously familiar; though how this could have occurred remained unknown.

This fascination with attributed and elective gender was to be significant, both for Michael and me in later years, when we came to write plays which were, in fact, projections of a kind of intense and unself-conscious drag-act we had perfected, and which passed for social realism. This form of therapy lasted twenty years, highly entertaining for us, if less so for any audience it may have attracted.

Although both inhabited by the spirit of our mothers, these were inflected by our highly competitive selves; perhaps the residue of our years of exposure to a grammar school which offered intensive tutelage, although it appeared in no curriculum, in both snobbery and social ambition. We were told that we were among the top 0.1 percent of the population in intelligence; a proposition we found it difficult to disavow, for all our rejection of the idea of a pyramidal social hierarchy, of which the brightest and best would surely find their way to the top. Flattery often pulls the sting of criticism; and this was skilfully practised by those entrusted with our educational formation. We disbelieved almost everything we were told; but the idea that we were distinguished by our intellectual capacity was too compelling for us to resist.

This competitive quality was illuminated by the fact that we both received an Exhibition at Cambridge. We did not, of course, know what that meant, since the only time we had ever heard the word was when we had been – not infrequently – accused as children of 'making an exhibition of ourselves'. We were to understand that this was a significant honour in admission to Cambridge. When I received a telegram some days before Christmas, I urgently communicated this to Michael. Dejected, he assumed that he had been passed over, and I spent a day exulting secretly in what I thought might be a recognition of my superiority. When Michael was informed he had achieved the equivalent next day, I was somewhat mortified. I did not find much comfort when Michael's mother suggested that his accomplishment might be inferior to mine, because he had received news of it a day later.

಼ಲ ಛ

The excursion to Cambridge, where we were interviewed, tested academically and socially for our right to be educated in that exalted institution, was also deeply instructive; although we had some idea of what was required of us.

Michael recounted his interview in detail. The tutor, a man of some humour beneath his austere demeanour, began:

'Come in, Mr O'Neill. I have read your paean of praise to the working classes with great pleasure. From where did you plagiarise it?'

'I didn't. I was only describing the way my family live.'

'It's a delightful polemic. Only you make – where is it? – Northampton sound like pre-revolutionary Smolensk. Do people really spit on the buses?'

'Well yes, they do. At each other more often than not.'

'And is goose-grease really considered a specific against pulmonary ailments?'

'Yes. And we also keep jars of mature urine for outbreaks of warts.'

The tutor guffawed. Michael, becoming heated, said, 'Why is it so funny? Only nine years ago people were still dying of TB because they couldn't afford to go to a doctor. They had to rely on self-medication.'

'Well, perhaps there are more similarities between Northampton and Smolensk than I had thought. Do you like your sherry dry?'

'No, actually I prefer it medium.'

'I suppose that is also a working-class habit.'

I sat in a seventeenth-century antechamber, waiting to enter the panelled study where I, too, had resolved to flaunt my working-class credentials. There were two other candidates. One had his feet on the coffee table and the other was tipping backwards on what I thought, no doubt mistakenly, was a valuable Sheraton chair.

'Well of course I don't know whether I am going to be frightfully popular here. After all, my grandfather did burn down the reredos and sixteen pews in chapel when he fell asleep smoking a cigar. Medieval, I believe it was. Quite irreplaceable.'

'Well for me it was touch and go between here and the Sorbonne. But frankly I didn't relish the pox from all those grubby French whores.'

Not wishing to appear stand-offish, I ventured that I thought it was going to be enriching, mixing with people from different backgrounds.

'God, what a ghastly person.'

'Where I come from you have to be introduced before you make banal remarks, and as I'm sure we have no acquaintance in common, it's unlikely we ever shall be.'

The tutor's voice summoned me at that point. 'Jeremy Seabrook. Northampton Grammar School.' My companions laughed. As I stood up, the seat of the chair stuck to my trousers, and it fell with a thud behind me.

'They've all got sticky arses, these grammar grubs. Never learn to wipe 'em properly.'

Michael and I were fortunate in a way. This was the time when it was fashionable to be working class; in particular, male and working class. Society, apparently fickle with its favours, has an acute sense of its own self-preservation, and recognises which groups need to be conciliated at any given time in the interests of maintaining social peace. Later, it would be women; then gay men and lesbians; later still, ethnic minorities; and each time the group elevated would be displayed as evidence, not only of humanitarian sentiment but also of social progress.

Not only was this good luck for us, but we − or rather Michael − knew how to play the game; and I was grateful for his wisdom. He said we should be assertive but not quite aggressive. We should suggest a smouldering sulkiness. We should be earthy but not offensive. He carried it off far better than I could; but my pallid mimicry of his acting skills apparently served its purpose.

හ ශ

Although we sensed that our admission into the sacred groves of power was the result of chance, a moment when it was thought prudent to raise up some of the clever progeny of a class which had largely been denied the education which our parents had longed for, we did not let this interfere with our sense that this was only our due. After that Christmas we sat in the parlour till late at night. The later we sat, the more limitless our future appeared. Sometimes my mother would come in. She would linger, as though waiting to be included in something. But we fell silent. She thought we might rekindle her old love of George Eliot, Elizabeth Gaskell, Charlotte Bronte. We didn't. We just waited for her to go away again. Sometimes she might say, 'I can hold a conversation you know.'

'We're not holding conversations,' Michael said coldly, 'we're just talking.'

'I don't know what you can find to talk about all the time. It's a mystery to me. You sit here all hours. It's making you morbid, Jerry. I don't know about you Michael, but iron tonic and plenty of rest is what he needs.'

Occasionally, unable to bear it any longer, she would come in at one o'clock in the morning, in her dressing gown and pyjamas, her hair in its thinning night-time pig-tail. She would say, 'Bugger off, O'Neill, if you've got a home to go to. And you, Jerry, get upstairs. Your hot water bottle's gone stone cold.'

Michael would say, 'It's all right. I'll go and sleep in the park till morning. I've forgotten my key. And if I wake them up, I'll get a beating.'

Although she sometimes showed exasperation with Michael, and sometimes used his apparently neglected condition as a warning, contrasted to the loving care bestowed on me, she often colluded with him over my dependency and fecklessness – qualities she had done so much to foster. 'You'll never amount to much,' she would say, 'you've got nothing about you, you're not half as sharp as Michael. The artful little bugger, he knows ten more tricks than a monkey.'

In a more serious mood, she would occasionally wonder what would happen to me when she was no longer there to take care of me. Once, she even said to Michael, 'Make sure he's all right when I'm not here, won't you Michael?' To this undertaking he solemnly agreed; but I was humiliated, fearful of what he would say when we were alone together. He was scornful. 'I hope she doesn't write it into her will. What would I want with you as a human hereditament? I couldn't even exchange you for hard cash.' I was anxious, less because of the ridicule than of the betrayal of an emotional weakness we had combined to place under prohibition.

Secretly, we both knew the elaborate pose we extended into adult life was a fiction; but since Michael derived greater advantage from it than I did, he was more committed to it than I was. And as time passed, I had an ally who could not have been more antagonistic to the brittle façade of uncaring we had created.

ഔ ଓଃ

This was Janet. She proved to know more about us than we ourselves knew, and as such became the first agent in the dissolution of the collusive bondage that had tethered Michael and me together. Her understanding of the world was of a different order from that which Michael and I had conceived. She became a loving and loyal friend, qualities which presented a seductive challenge to the icy numbness of my attachment to Michael. They never liked each other.

We had met at the drama club we organised in the sixth form. Wanting to escape the pedestrian and all-male establishment of school, designed for the sons of local business families to maintain their social position through the inherited business of gentlemen's outfitter or timber merchant to even more dazzling heights, we took refuge in the theatre.

Michael and I, and some other friends, asked some girls from the fee-paying school to join an extra-curricular club. We had no expectation that they would accept; but on the first evening, six young women appeared before our dazzled senses, and Janet danced into our lives – a vortex of colour and emotion. Under the influence of a charismatic teacher, her heart was still in the Spanish Civil War, and she quoted Lorca with a flawless accent until the tears ran down her cheeks. Hers was a poetic leftism, an instinctive attraction to the defenceless and the vanquished of history. She was a passionate advocate on behalf of the Third World, long before any such expression had even been uttered in that sequestered provincial place. Through her and her friends, we read plays of an extraordinary range – *Cymbeline* and *Titus Andronicus*, Racine's *Phèdre*, Calderón, Lorca, Elroy-Flecker's *Hassan*, John Masefield's *Tragedy of Nan*, Sophocles, Aristophanes, John Millington Synge, Christopher Fry, Pirandello, Molière, Webster, Beaumont and Fletcher.... There was nothing in the theatre with which they were not familiar. How was it possible we had never heard of most of them?

The evenings, apparently glamourless and functional in the basement of the town's Liberal Club, were full of enchantment, as our intense, repressed feelings found an outlet in the safe, though elevating, words of others. When the play reading was over, the watery coffee and thin arrowroot biscuits gone, the caretaker rattled his bucket and keys as a signal that our tenure of the space was over, we would saunter to the nearby churchyard, and sit on marble tombstones sacred to the memory of Frederick Ephraim Klitz and sparkling with frost, as Janet declaimed Rimbaud and Mallarmé in a boletus of visible breath, and we shivered, waiting, but not willing for the recital to finish. She would declaim, '*O lune triste et pale qui éteint les étoiles ...*'

'That's Baudelaire isn't it?'

'I wrote it myself last night,' she would say. 'I'm more influenced by Verlaine.'

Michael said, 'Janet, you'll get piles, sitting on that cold marble.'

Michael did not like Janet. He thought her ethereal and unrealistic, which she was. Although generous and impulsive herself, she never had any money and lived equably in the material space provided by others. But Michael's real objection to her was that she threatened to unlock whatever was sequestered in our steely adolescent breasts. Yet she was to become, and to remain, a constant presence in our lives until she died; and it is thanks to her healing influence that we finally broke free from the disorder of our petrified – in both senses – relationship.

Waiting for Janet in the cold was to become a habit. Later, during our first term at Cambridge, on Poppy Day she dressed herself as a mermaid, which involved letting down her hair, wearing a top of mock seaweed and forcing her legs into a constricting fish-tail sparkling with sequin-scales. This made it impossible for her to walk, so we carried her all day in the freezing gale, collecting in the process a phenomenal sum of money.

The girls brought by Janet into our drama circle exercised over the boys – all working-class and almost all gay, as it turned out – a double fascination. They were all from professional middle-class families, and they offered us the chance to define, not only our social origins, but also our sexuality, in the presence of their collective charm, poise and power. If we imagined erotic possibilities, we knew we would not have to put them into practice; a hesitancy which only made more puzzling the question of *what they saw in us*. How could we have suspected that we might appear as exotic to them as they did to us? Yet such was the temper of that joyless era, that boys emerging from shabby streets and austere estates, could be objects of mystery to those who had been raised in villas in the genteel parts of town, accustomed to tea-time with tiered cake-stands in tepid conservatories, schooled in fine arts and literature, and educated in establishments designed to produce young ladies, a category from which they were as anxious for escape as we were from our low origins. When they discovered that those issuing from such sombre proletarian haunts could be intelligent, amusing and have the allure of a *beau ténébreux* to eyes that had, until then, seen only the hearty, extrovert rugby-playing friends of their dull brothers, they found much to admire. No more implausible seduction could be imagined than that each group saw in the other something alluring and magical. Of course, the barriers that divided class from class in that time of airtight social segregation have long been, if not demolished, at least ruptured sufficiently to make a passage through them far easier than it then appeared. But we saw ourselves as pathfinders, colonial explorers in a way, in search of uncontacted cultures concealed from view by the dense forests of provincial prejudice.

Janet appealed to us because of her desire to transcend Northampton, as well as the series of leaky manses in other provincial exiles, in which she had been brought up. She also wanted to rise above the parochialism of a Britain which still asserted a global imperial reach; and at that time French and Spanish literature were the most immediately accessible vehicles for her flights. Anyone willing to accompany her was more than welcome. Under her influence I carried a copy of Sartre's *La Nausée*, with the title conspicuously turned to public view; a gesture which I doubt anyone in Northampton ever noticed.

Janet invited us to her home, a draughty rectory on the edge of town, where, in winter, snow came through the faulty leaded lights and accumulated in small drifts on the window-sill. Laurels obstructed the gloomy daylight, and spindly mushrooms grew in the corners of the ceiling.

'Darlings, come to my Turkish party on Saturday. I'm turning Daddy's study into the court of Mohammed II.'

'What do we wear?' I asked anxiously.

Michael said, 'I'll come as a janissary. They were Christian boys, kidnapped, circumcised and brought up by eunuchs.'

The rectory was illuminated with candles. There was incense and Mozart's *Rondo Alla Turca* was playing. Janet said, 'Darlings, you look super.' I had taken one of my mother's frocks, a black crepe de chine dress with appliquéd moons and stars. I said, 'I hope she doesn't find out. She once gave me a good hiding for dressing up in her clothes.' Michael said scornfully, 'That was transvestism. This is fancy dress.'

Andrea asked 'Do you think I am a better slave girl than Janet? I'm much more submissive.'

'Actually, I'm an odalisque.'

'We had one of those in the field behind our house. Or was that an obelisk?'

Janet said crossly, 'We're in Turkey. Northampton no longer exists. We are by the jasmine-scented Bosphorus, and the air is heavy with musky scent and human desire. Mohammed II is holding court in the Hagia Sofia. We're going to torture Michael, because he is a captured Byzantine patriarch. He's to be converted to Islam.'

Andrea took up the theme, 'I shall tickle his feet with an ostrich feather until he can bear it no longer.'

'And Gillian is going to make him mad with desire.'

'I think that's even beyond me,' said the knowing Gillian.

Michael was held down and tortured by the girls. Janet's father appeared in the doorway, in his clerical collar. He was large and florid with tufts of white hair on either side of his head. He entered into the spirit of the entertainment with enthusiasm. 'Pon my soul, infidels in the heart of Christendom. Unexampled heterodoxy. Islam raging in the drawing-room of an English rectory. Should this come to the ears of the bishop, I should almost certainly be anathematised.'

I whispered to Michael, 'That's the vicar.' Michael said, 'It's her dad.'

'Darling Daddy, do join us,' cried Janet. The Reverend Ashworth wrapped an antimacassar round his head and sat cross-legged on a cushion. 'Oh Scheherazade, woe unto you if you cannot beguile my weary spirit with a story tonight. If you fail, your lovely head will adorn the city gates for the delectation of the vultures.'

Janet fell onto her knees. 'O Caliph, spare me. I shall tell you the tale of the merchant travelling from Samarkand.' Michael interrupted, 'Haven't we gone a bit astray? I thought we were in Turkey.'

'Don't be so prosaic Michael. I am going to tell the story of the merchant and the mendicant – how the man of commerce found his humanity through a beggar. Then Daddy is going to read to us from the Koran and teach us some chants. Then we shall eat lambs' sweetbreads with mint and yaourt.'

Michael said, 'You know what sweetbreads are? I'm not touching that.'

The evening finished with Michael singing 'The Maharajah of Magador':

He had rubies and pearls,
and the loveliest girls,
But he didn't know how to do the rumba …

ℬ ℭ

Janet, at fifteen, was instructor and guide. She taught me that learning languages had nothing to do with conjugation or irregular subjunctives, as our teachers had solemnly declared; but poetry and literature, which were to her a means of conveyance out of the provincial town, a barouche or phaeton rather than a bus or train, to destinations that didn't matter as long as they were elsewhere. She had long ago learned the importance of running away. As a child, she had been plump and moon-faced, and had spent long hours weeping in the glebe among the Madonna lilies for the beauty she longed for.

And which she did, indeed, attain. She had a wide face and broad forehead; her hair was fair and fine, and her eyes, embracing a world from which she expected only good things, were grey and vulnerable. By showing how easily she could be wounded, she defied others to hurt her; which they rarely did. She attracted by her refusal to judge and her readiness to accept people's account of themselves. She invited confidences. Women on the bus would turn to her, and say of their husband, 'He hasn't touched me for twenty-five years,' or of their son, 'He's a wrong'un, pity he never finished up flushed down the pan like the others.' Janet was never shocked. It was not an accident that many of her friends were gay men; nor that, as she grew weaker in the long illness that would take her life, we were among the most loyal. Sometimes we took her to the theatre, in which at that time, there was little provision for wheelchairs, and we lifted her into her seat in the front row of the stalls. We saw *King Lear*, Anouilh's *Antigone* and the Comédie-Française production of *Phèdre*. At the end of the performance her face would be wet with the tears she had shed, not only for the protagonists in the play or for herself, but also for the sufferings of others, into which her capacity for imaginative compassion always permitted her to enter.

Objectively, Janet was an unlikely symbol of escape. She could not have been more different from the austere faded rectitude often associated with the Anglican clergyman, of whom her father was scarcely typical. He was an expansive and highly literate man, in his way also a dreamer, kindly, other-worldly, serene and slightly florid. His wife was the power in the family: capable, practical, blessed with a tolerant sense of irony; as different from her daughter as could be imagined. Indeed, Janet lost her faith in adolescence; a lapse she was careful to conceal from her parents for the rest of her life, since, tender-hearted, she had no wish to trouble the serenity of their belief. Both outlived her. Her scepticism became extremely difficult, since she spent the last years of her life in the British Home and Hospital for Incurables in Streatham, a place redolent of Victorian philanthropy and slightly punitive condescension, where some of the staff took – and gave – grim lessons in Christian fortitude, and treated some of the patients, already in the last throes of debilitating sickness, as if they – the staff – were living testimonies to the goodness of God, since he had guided his servants to take care of the unfortunates destined to waste away in the stony enclosure of that institution.

But that was a long time in the future. We decided that we would show Northampton the meaning of drama. The young women knew a play (how?) called *Happy and Glorious*, about the disillusionment and guilt of survivors of the First World War. Written by a man still living, Janet decided we would visit him in his home in Hampstead Garden Suburb. I was horrified. You don't invite yourself to the homes of authors. They are too busy, too important. They wouldn't have time for the likes of us.

'Rubbish,' said the girls, for him Calderón and Goldoni were as familiar as the ice-cream vendors whose names they evoked were to us. 'Of course we'll see him, talk to him about the play and his thoughts on war, and the bitterness of the couple he has written about, who are unable to love after the exaltations and traumas of war. We will ask him if he wrote from personal experience.' The writer, Wilfred Walter, was a charming elderly man, delighted to receive four of us in his chintzy parlour, where he offered us tea and toasted crumpets, quite overcome that young people should have been sufficiently stirred to want to perform a play which had not been performed professionally since the Second World War, but had fallen into what he modestly called 'deserved obscurity'. He was deeply touched by our interest, but it was probably as well that he was too frail to attend, since our production was scarcely flawless.

It was played in the Co-Op Hall, an impressive auditorium above the white-and-green-tiled store close to the centre of town, which still retained an aura of community sharing and distribution of the 'divvy' to its members. This was the 1950s, and we were animated by a mission to bring to the people our vision of a world more cultured than that of dog-racing, corner pub and picture-house. At that time, it seemed, everybody (at least Arnold Wesker) was reaching out to a working class which was, to us, the more elusive, for being alive and well and sitting at home listening to *Educating Archie* and *Life with the Lyons*.* We sold tickets to family and friends, and their friends and families. My role was that of embittered soldier, while Janet played the Parisian tart, slinky and seductive, the soldier's encounter with whose kindly tolerance had spoilt him for the wholesome fiancée who could no longer reach him with her promise of domesticity, gardening and babies.

Emboldened by a favourable review in the local paper, we decided to have another go at raising the cultural tone of the

---

* These entertainments seem strange to posterity. *Educating Archie* involved ventriloquist and his dummy ON THE RADIO, while *Life with the Lyons* was a bland sit-com with the real family of Bebe Daniels, a US musical theatre star of the pre-war years.

town by producing *Othello*, for which I was the natural (that is, only) choice of lead. I assumed my second out-of-character martial role. In the 1950s, 'blacking-up' had not yet been discredited; so a liberal application of Cherry Blossom boot polish was the only agent of transformation required. Janet played Emilia; and I can still hear the passion in her eighteen-year-old voice:

'And have we not affections,

Desires for sport, and frailty, as men have?

Then let them use us well; else let them know

The ills we do their ills instruct us to.'

The *éclat* we imagined we had created in Northampton seemed a prelude to Cambridge when Janet's place at Girton was confirmed.

୫ ଓ

I pretended to share Michael's excitement at the prospect of Cambridge. We sat in the parlour for the last time, as my mother counted out the Chilprufe vests she had bought from the best Gentlemen's Outfitters in town, and the thick socks she had knitted. She offered advice on table manners – her grandfather had, after all, been in service, and had taught her such elementary customs as starting with the cutlery on the outside of the table setting; lessons for feasts she was never likely to attend, but which she thought useful to pass on to me. She could have known no more about the prevailing mood at dinner in hall, where significant portions of the comestibles – pellets of bread and the occasional Brussels sprout – would be flicked as missiles across the tables before lodging themselves in some medieval timbering, than she could of the wretched fare, gristle and lumpy potatoes and syrupy stodge moistened with watery custard – a diet which had more in common with that of the workhouse, an institution with which the family

103

were, in folk-memory, on far more familiar terms than with college banquets.

Our parents wanted the impossible of us: they wanted us to rise in the world but not to get above ourselves; a sort of metaphysical levitation, in which we would remain ourselves yet belong to a higher caste. Michael's mother bought him a silk dressing gown. He said, 'I don't want a dressing gown.' 'You've got to have a dressing gown Michael, to show you come from a family that's used to lounging about in the mornings.' A moment later she would be admonishing him not to forget she had scrubbed floors to give him the chances she never had.

Michael goaded my mother, when she tried to imagine the golden future that beckoned us. 'All I want is a garret and lots of people. I can live on bread crusts and cheap wine. We can roll around the world with holes in our pockets.' She said sharply, 'Jerry, I don't want you being no Bohemian.' Michael sang a few bars of *Che Gelida Manina*, an aria from *La Bohème*. 'That isn't the way I've brought him up.'

'That's the way he's going though.'

'Over my dead body.'

'You've got to go sometime.'

She turned to me. 'Jerry. I want you to swear a solemn oath to me.'

'What Mum?'

'That you won't start any loose living. After the way I've sacrificed myself, walking through the world, a woman on her own.'

'No, Mum.'

She turned in triumph to Michael. 'So you can speak for yourself in future O'Neill.... Now finish up that fruit salad.'

When she had left the room Michael said to me, 'You bloody hypocrite.'

'She's had a rotten life Michael.'

'So did Little Nell.'

I was driven to Cambridge in Uncle Arthur's Ford Cortina, my trunk – donated by Miss Wood next door – carefully secured in the boot, containing six Denby ware cups, saucers and plates, my winter clothes and a Victoria sponge made by my aunt and tenderly wrapped in tissue paper. My arrival was timidly decorous, but Michael knew (how?) that in Cambridge at that time there was a brisk trade in awkward proletarians; and had arrived well prepared for that role, with muffler, lace-up boots and flat cap which he wore at a winsome angle. He actually would have passed for an Edwardian waif and was far better at it than most other pretenders to this then-fashionable identity. He soon discovered that some of the college servants were Teddy-boys, and he invited them into his room to listen to Elvis records. This lent him an air of authenticity, which, he said, turned certain public school boys green with envy; although Michael admitted the acquaintance-ship of boys from the Fens was not very stimulating. They would say, 'Cool platter, Mick,' and he would ask them why they were speaking phoney American when they could as well have expressed themselves in English. They asked each other, 'What does he want us round here for? Is he a queer?' 'He don't half throw his money around. They say he owns half of Scotland, and that his mum and dad live in a castle.'

The undergraduates said to Michael, 'Golly, Michael. You do get on with them. I wish you'd teach me how to talk to them.' Michael said, 'I'll give you elocution lessons.'

Next day, there was a social call of a different kind. Michael was sweeping up the beer bottles, when there came a knock at the door. It was the wife of the Master or some other figure of Authority.

Without preamble, she said sternly, 'We do not normally have to draw the attention of gentlemen to the rules of the college concerning their conduct towards servants. Such knowledge is generally known as a result of good breeding. One does not invite them into one's room for social purposes.'

'Oh, I do. I find their company more stimulating.'

'Indeed. Then I suggest you re-apply for admission to the college by way of the kitchens. I'm sure that will suit your no doubt considerable talents equally well.'

Michael loved it. Meanwhile I had taken my smothered feelings and suppressed sexuality with me and brooded over them like a bird sitting on addled eggs. Michael maintained the (for him) fiction that life in Cambridge was awful, that he hated it and could not wait for it to be over, so that he could get on with his life. The expression of his apparent dissatisfaction drew from me a confession of my real unhappiness. He listened sympathetically but could not stay long because he was expected elsewhere. He would come cheerfully into my room. 'Hello Jerry. What you doing, reading something exciting?'

'Oh hello. It's Foscolo.'

'Who the fuck's Foscolo?'

'Dei Sepolcri. Sepulchres.'

'I don't know how you can do it.'

'You're bright and breezy.'

'Breezy but not very bright.'

'What have you been doing?'

'You know me, you know how boring my life is.'

'I don't know Michael.'

'No. What have I got in my life? I've got no friends. I can't keep up with the essays. Do you know anything about cross-cousin marriage among the Nuer? All I know is that they stretch their pricks and divine their future through the chief's turds.'

'Good a way as any.'

'My room is cold.... It has a microclimate. It's foggy. I don't know, I don't seem to get on with anyone. Nobody seems to like me very much.'

I responded to his apparent candour. 'I know how you feel. I haven't spoken to anyone since Sunday.'

'You must have.'

'I might have said thank you to the lady in the bakery.... You see that window in the gate tower? The boy who lived there committed suicide on Tuesday He gassed himself.'

'Yes, we've had three in Queen's this term. Or is it four?'

'I can understand it, you know.... If I had known him, I would have done something.... Can you imagine, the state of someone's mind just before he does something like that?'

'Yeh. Still. I saw a smashing film last night.'

'Oh.'

'Yeh. It was called *La Strada*. You'd've loved it.'

'Why do you go to the pictures on your own then?'

'I didn't. I went with one or two people from King's.

'Oh.'

'I met them at a party. I think they sniff cocaine. But I didn't.'

'So what was the film like?'

'It was beautiful. This girl, she's a bit simple and she attaches herself to this man in a travelling circus who really treats her like shit. It's really moving. He looks on her as a burden, but as time goes by, he becomes dependent on her.'

'I might go to see it.'

'Pity I've already been. Oh well. I've got to go to a seminar on voodoo. I'll pop in later in the week, see how you are.' This made me feel like an invalid. Michael went, slamming the door and calling, 'Don't get too buried in the sepulchres.' I sometimes thought he was protecting me from people. He really saw how awful I was and was being kind by sequestering me from the world. Then at other times, I felt he was colluding

107

with my — what was it, shyness, sense of inferiority, fear? — which prevented me from meeting anyone else.

⁊ ⳗ

I was very unhappy and terrified of people, particularly of those who were so self-confident and whose voices bounced like cannon-balls off the stonework of the college courtyard. If I dared to approach anyone, I thought the conversation would go like this. I would timidly say, 'Excuse me ... but do you think Proust really conquered time, or did he just imagine he did?' The undergraduate I had addressed would reply, 'How dare you talk to me? I can see through you. You're worthless, vain and futile, and ugly with it. So don't come blubbering to me, using the greatest artists of our century as a pretext.' How much better, it seemed to me, not to risk such humiliating rebuffs by avoiding all contact.

Janet, meanwhile, was enjoying a different kind of success. She was soon at the centre of a group of girls from all over the world; among them, a Nigerian heiress, a relative of the Thai royal Indian family, an Iranian scientist who was related to the Shah, a woman whose family had fled Hungary after the Soviet invasion. She invited Michael and me to tea. Our working-class exoticism had clearly been eclipsed by the fabulous places from which her friends came.

Phailin, the Thai princess, said, 'Michael. Janet tells me your parents live in extraordinary poverty. I wonder if I could do anything to help them.' Michael, irritated, replied, 'Haven't you got rather a lot of poverty in Thailand, if you've money to spare?' 'No Michael. The Thai is stupid and lazy and will not do anything to help himself.'

Janet tactfully intervened, 'Michael, darling, have another chocolate ant. I gave them to Yomi for a birthday present.' Yomi said, 'It was the most exciting gift. I got some boring presents from my father. Just think. He gave me a hospital for my birthday.' Michael asked disagreeably, 'Complete with lepers?' 'Why is that boring?' I wondered. 'He gave me the same thing last year. I don't know what I shall do with it. I think I shall send all the people away and turn it into a luxury hotel.'

Janet urged us all to sit cross-legged on the floor to eat the meal from the Maghreb she had prepared. 'I followed the recipe, but it should be cooked over camel dung; only there aren't too many camels in Girton.' Michael muttered that he could see at least three. 'Now honeys,' she lilted, 'Stir it round. It's called *tchektchouka*.' Michael said 'It looks like sick.'

There was a moment of silence. Then Janet said, 'I hate you. I hate you. You've ruined my supper party. If you're going to be such a horrible trog, you should have stayed in damned Northampton.'

We didn't see much of her friends after that; although many years later, I saw Phailin's name when she put herself forward as Conservative candidate for an unwinnable seat in Manchester.

This further reduced my already limited circle of acquaintances. Michael told me later that he pretended to be miserable in my company because he thought it was a pose, my version of his angry proletarian youth. If he shunned me for much of the time, this was because he found it a strain to pretend to be unhappy when he was having the time of his life. He was unaware that what he saw as my fashionable nihilism was not a mask to conceal my deep unhappiness. He asked me how I expected him to see through that. 'I didn't. But I thought if this is friendship, what does real indifference look like?'

Many years afterwards, I asked Michael to tell me what the good time he was having looked like.

He said, 'Imagine a dinner party. Some highly serious undergraduate would say "Well, of course, the marvellous thing about working with pre-literate peoples is the incredible richness and variety of the oral tradition. We have totally lost that in England.'" Michael said, 'Not where I come from.' 'Oh, really?' 'Yeh. My dad taught me all sorts of oral traditions – cunnilingus, fellatio, rimming.' The room erupted with laughter.

When Michael went on his sexual adventures, in Cambridge, and increasingly, in London, he set out to be gauche, monosyllabic and slightly brutal. It worked like a charm. He called himself Spike, a nickname he had learned in Northampton, to enhance an aura of rough masculinity. He was picked up in the Coleherne, a gay pub in West London, by an artist called Miles, who took him to a palatial flat in South Kensington.

Michael looked at the paintings on the wall. Miles was nervous at the bit of rough he had brought home and was wondering if he had acted too precipitately. 'The one you're looking at is a Braque. Do you like Braque?' Michael mumbled, 'Yeh.' 'Post-Cubist of course. That is an original. I gave the sweetest little creature two hundred cigarettes for it after the Liberation.' 'Yeh.' Miles, increasingly desperate, asked, 'What kind of paintings do you prefer?' 'I like photos.' 'Come now … I'm sure you'd prefer … let me see, looking at you … a Kokoschka.'

'Michael said, 'Talking of cocks, I need a piss.'

'Oh yes, of course. Through there.' As soon as Michael had gone into the bathroom, Miles lifted the phone. Michael could hear the conversation through the door, 'Hello, Guy, is that you? Look, darling could you do me a favour, get over here at once … I've got a prole here, terribly attractive, but brutal…. Jump in a taxi, sweetie, as I rather value my skull.'

At the time, I had no idea that such encounters were taking place. I nursed a secret passion for a boy in college, with whom I scarcely exchanged a dozen words. I had already gone through enough of these unreciprocated relationships, if that is what they were. I consoled myself with the thought that Dante had only ever seen Beatrice once on the banks of the Arno, so my one-way passions might not ultimately prove unproductive. Michael would have been contemptuous of such adolescent regression, so I never mentioned it, as a detail scarcely worthy of recall.

For me, the most of the rare redeeming moments in Cambridge involved Janet. Although she, too, made an independent life for herself in Cambridge, she had a genuine capacity for friendship, which she took seriously. She was never unavailable or too busy. Girton, for her, meant sitting in sisterly commiseration until three in the morning with the heartbroken and the unloved, waiting for her own beau to climb secretly into the fortified women's college, to be with her until dawn broke over the fenny fields, when he would decamp, undetected, hair and scarf flying in the wind.... Cambridge was also where you discovered who you really were. And whether the liberal values of your old teachers would withstand the rigorous challenges to which they would now be subjected, or whether you would leave them behind as youthful folly, and come to a mature acceptance that the society which had lavished its prizes upon you was indeed the culmination of human civilisation; in favour of which view all the evidence had been carefully assembled in advance – the fine architecture, expensive college silver, grace spoken in Latin, and history seated everywhere in erudite judgement on the delinquencies of posterity.

As a distraction from these absorbing issues, Janet always had time to see me. I remember one June day, we went for a picnic in a field of tall dry grasses. It was cool and breezy, but the shelter we made in the sedge created a nest of warmth and stillness. We did nothing the whole afternoon but recite fragments of French poetry that had attracted us: '*Le vierge, le vivace et le bel aujourd'hui ...*'; or '*Je suis le ténébreux, le veuf, l'inconsole …*'. We picked some wild flowers – butter-cups, purple clover, herb Robert, white and red dead-nettle and yellow loosestrife, which I later placed on the table in my Spartan room. The sight of them made me cry with an instant nostalgia for the sweetness of the spent summer afternoon. Janet had the gift of always being totally present, wherever she was; she never hankered to be elsewhere or wondered what more exciting company she might be missing. And when she spoke, her eyes looked at you at a sherry-party or some other unwelcome social ritual and were never glancing over your shoulder to see if there might be more important people to cultivate. The joy she took in simply existing remained a mystery to me. I wanted her to teach me to be happy; but that lay beyond even her considerable powers of instruction. She did, however, by her very presence, free me from the oppressively competitive relationship with Michael. And he always knew when Janet and I had been together since I always exuded a faint hostility towards him. He would say something particularly disparaging about her; and although I resisted, it was a muted protest, easily swept away.

Janet never criticised Michael. This was, in any case, unnecessary, since her warmth and affection spoke to me eloquently against the chill ritual of my friendship with him. What I had regarded as the shameful secret of my sexuality was known to her without any avowal; and she spoke as though she had always known it. When the alleged 'causes' of homosexuality were publicly spoken about at that time, it was widely assumed that 'possessive mothers' played a crucial role. Janet saw that this was absurd. She said, 'Certain sensibilities in boys are drawn towards women, and it is this, and the relationship between mothers and sons is a result of sexual orientation, not a cause of it.' Michael would say to her, 'What do you know about it?' She answered, 'Oh nothing. Nothing at all.'

Janet had her own first romantic relationship in Cambridge; a beautiful Indian boy who was badly hurt by a fall in the Cam, and who was forced by his family to break off the relationship with Janet. It was after this that the malignancy which had been biding its time in her elegant body began to stir and make its – unsuccessful – effort to conquer her spirit. Janet had always moved with a studied emphatic grace, as though, even in her youth, she was conscious of resistance against the internal assailant. At her twenty-first birthday party at Girton, she was at her most radiant in a green-blue dress, with long silver earrings and her hair tied in a loose skein that filled with light as she moved. If she seemed a little unsteady on her high heels, this might well have been as a result of the compliments she had been paid, the many gifts from friends, too much *sangria* or the presence of luminaries from the French faculty – Dr Alison Fairlie and Odette de Mourgues. What had appeared to be the prelude to a life of glamour and distinction proved to be the high point of her life.

ഇ ൽ

In 1959, just before my final year at Cambridge, I spent the first part of the vacation on an intensive Italian course at the *Università per Stranieri* in Rome. I stayed in a gloomy *pensione* close to the Spanish Steps, and went daily for instruction to the classroom in a narrow street where trapped orange wedges of sunlight turned the upper storeys of buildings into aerial palaces, another, more magical city than the shadowed streets below.

I had a bursary from the Italian government and took very seriously the purposes for which it had been granted. Earnest and intense, I was astonished to discover that most of my fellow-students had a far more frivolous ambition – to get drunk, have fun and to lose their virginity, a primitively erotic venture in a pre-liberated time. I told myself I had come to the land of Dante and Petrarch, but in vain. The distractions of contemporary – fleshly – beauty simply erased all such thoughts from my mind. The light and heat of the city disturbed my mission of self-improvement; they promised experiences unavailable at home.

I had taken with me all the repressed longings which Michael had kindly helped me to keep in check. I knew that homosexuality was not a criminal offence on the continent, as it remained at home, and I hoped that *something would happen*. Accordingly, every day, after class, I installed myself on the steep stone slope of the balustrade at the top of the Spanish Steps, expecting much of a place in which, unknown, I could perhaps behave in ways I would never have dared, even in Cambridge, let alone at home in Northampton.

Opportunities were slow in coming. I looked searchingly into the eyes of passers-by. Too many of them had accents like Gracie Fields; women who walked in defensive groups and hugged their handbags to their bodies in anticipation of Italian pickpockets and cutpurses, against whom tour organisers had warned them to be on their guard.

One afternoon, when the city was flooded with molten gold and the heat discomposed the buildings on the other side of the Piazza di Spagna, a slim young man materialised out of the fumes and seated himself on the balustrade on the opposite side of the steps, in a posture unmistakeably symmetrical to my own. It was suffocatingly hot, desire and abandon in the air. My companion – for so I thought of him – smiled. His hair was a bronze colour, his skin pale and eyes so lucent they appeared to glow from within, like the candle in the hollowed out head of pumpkins at Hallowe'en. He was wearing a striped matelot's jersey and jeans, and I thought him the most beautiful creature I had ever seen.

He came over to talk to me. I answered him in Italian – the first useful conversation I had had in that melodious tongue, although he spoke with a sharp Roman accent. He asked me why I was alone, a question which appeared to me a thrilling preamble to a relationship, the nature of which I had no difficulty in imagining. This was confirmed by his next question. Do you have a girl friend? No. He did, it appeared, but she only wanted money. I ought, perhaps, to have been on my guard at this, but I was so enchanted that I was all candour and conspicuous admiration. He asked me if I liked girls. I said yes, but that I liked friendship with boys too. He said would you like me to be your friend. Of course. *Dovresti pagare*, he said, 'It will cost you.'

I understood then the nature of his calling. He wanted a thousand lire and the bracelet I was wearing. This was a showy piece of kitsch I had exchanged with Janet, an eternity love-bangle, and therefore to be bartered away at the first opportunity for dalliance. I had no difficulty in parting with it. A thousand lire, too, seemed a small price to pay for initiation into the mysteries of friendship with an Italian boy, who, I reflected, must have been younger than I was, no more than seventeen or eighteen.

We walked in tense silence, he leading the way into the Villa Borghese. We came to an alley bordered by dark flames of cypress trees, which burnt with a hot resinous scent. He put two fingers in his mouth and produced a shrill whistle. Out of nowhere, a child of maybe ten or eleven appeared. He told him to watch out for other walkers, and to be sure to whistle if he saw anyone approach. He then sat down, unzipped his fly and invited me to masturbate him.

This brief meeting was as close as I came to the amorous entanglements of my fellow-students. It was abridged by the sudden recollection that this was the afternoon of the examination, the diploma I would require in order to dislodge the bursary from its bureaucratic fastness. Hastily, I offered the gifts demanded and fled, so as not to miss the appointment with the examiner. In the rush, I failed to notice that as I sat on the grassy knoll, my shoe had rested in shit, human shit, richly dark and odorous.

I arrived, out of breath in the stifling heat, attended by a powerful whiff of excrement; perhaps the least favourable circumstances in which to show my mastery of Italian. Yet curiously, the encounter had lent me an unusual acuity of mind. The examiner – a middle-aged woman inclined, in any case, to be indulgent towards me – looked at me kindly, and told me in Italian I looked as though I had '*cresciuto in fretta in fretta*', grown up in a hurry, a not at all disagreeable assessment. She offered me a glass of water. I passed with distinction.

The boy had made an assignation for the following day, hinting at the possibility of more intimate relations; but after that first clumsy meeting, I naturally avoided both the Spanish Steps and the Villa Borghese. In any case, two days later, I returned to the *pensione*, to discover the money and travellers' cheques which I had negligently left on the table of my room, had vanished. I did not associate the robbery with the vision on the Spanish Steps. The *Signora* said that such a thing was impossible in a respectable establishment like hers. My trip was abruptly curtailed. At that time, there was no question of having money remitted from home – I had no bank account, and it proved impossible to advance payment from the bursary, which, in any case, would be cancelled by my non-attendance in classes. So I took the train to Paris, thence to London, arriving back in Northampton, not two months later, as I had planned, but a paltry and shaming three weeks after my ceremonious departure on an appropriately debased version of the Grand Tour.

ℰ℧ ℭ℞

In consolation for this disappointment, which pleased my mother mightily, for she had always declared, not without boastful sorrow, how shiftless I was, she suggested we might make use of the unendingly fine weather to spend a couple of weeks at the seaside. It would have been difficult to imagine a less satisfactory form of recuperation. For between my mother and myself lay heavy secrets which we could not confess to each other, but which impeded all communication; tied us into a subdued melancholy, and made of being together a loving irritant. I could no more talk to her of my sexual longings than she could have told me that the man I called father was unrelated to me.

It seemed a more reasonable excursion than my exotic encounters with the continent, on which I maintained – for my family – an inexplicable reticence, although I had to admit to carelessness in letting myself be robbed. Why had I not sought justice, restitution, gone to the police, complained to the authorities? I tried to explain that the authorities in Rome were unlike anything known in Northampton; and in any case, I had an obscure feeling that the meeting with the boy might have been coincidental with the disappearance of my goods from the *pensione*; and the last thing I wanted was for connections to be made where they might indeed, for all I knew, have existed. Italy was, at that time, just coming into prominence as a tourist destination. Until then, it had been associated in the provincial mind of our town with prisoners of war, who had passed our house each day, when I was a child, in crowded snub-nosed buses taking them to their place of labour. Then, they had been workers in the brickfields of Bedfordshire, small dark men from Calabria with moustaches and muscles and skin reddened by the heat of the kilns. Italians as models of irresistible sexuality, vying with each other to seduce pallid English *signorinas* – and even some *signores* – was still only a faint rumour of what they were to become.

It was decided we would go to Paignton in Devon. For my mother – who already suffered mildly from the agoraphobia that was to chain her indoors for the last fifteen years of her life – this was a major upheaval. Packing was an onerous labour of Sisyphus – no sooner had every last thing been packed than it all had to be taken out again to make sure that some trivial item had not been omitted. And the departure itself was a scarcely tolerable burden. How many times the gas-taps had to be tested to make sure they were in the off position, with what effort the water pipe had to be closed, so that the pipes should not burst during an August heatwave; how discreetly the note to the milkman not to deliver had to be concealed beneath the bottle on the step. For my mother, every leave-taking, the most modest excursion or departure from home, always fore-shadowed something more final.

She had booked us into a boarding-house recommended by a neighbour – clean, good wholesome fare at reasona-ble prices. We carried our luggage like refugees, 'crossing London' at that time having something of the epic proper-ties of traversing the Alps. We asked directions several times, but always of the most inoffensive-looking people, because everyone knew London was full of thieves and vagabonds, and we wore our provincial status, not in our clothing, but in the perspiring anxiety of our faces, and the mystified gaze we turned upon conflicting signs and notices. The trouble with begging instruction of the harmless was that these often turned out to be, either strangers like ourselves, or of infirm understanding, so that little reliability could be placed in the information they gave us.

The train from Paddington was hot and crowded, since holidays at that time still retained awkward associations with wartime evacuation: luggage was piled high in the corridors, and some people still conveyed their belongings by trunk, padlocked metal caskets, which railway personnel accepted as part of their duty to carry from the train to taxi or whatever conveyance their owners used to get themselves to their hotel.

We walked to our boarding-house, about ten minutes from the station, in an Edwardian avenue of detached houses, most of them transformed into holiday hotels with names from elsewhere – Braemar or Capri, St Brelade's or Trouville. Hanging baskets of geraniums, pebble-dashed walls, hydrangeas and crazy paving welcomed us to the particular site of hospitality we had chosen. Inside it was clean but fussy, with pink velvet curtains, rosy wallpaper, warming-pans, Toby-jugs and pictures of Pussycats and Mabel Lucie Atwell children on the walls. The motif of the carpets suggested whirlpools of blood, while boughs of plastic lilac gushed from what looked like funerary urns.

We were just in time for the evening meal, which proved to be a sparing feast, although the napery was clean and white, and late sunshine through the laburnums superimposed another pattern upon the rose-bower wall. Five guineas a week bought an exquisite gentility, suppressed coughs and microscopic talk from the guests, who appeared stricken by the fear that anything they said might give offence. My mother and I sat in constrained silence, waiting for the poached egg on toast garnished with a round of tomato. I think we both knew immediately that this excursion was a terrible mistake. We behaved to each other with excruciating politeness, and exchanged details of our provenance with fellow-boarders – a major and his lady who had recently returned from Cyrenaica in Libya where, we learned, they was a British military base; an elderly couple from Chorley, which sounded like a jolly place, although if it were, it had communicated to them no trace of its gaiety, and a lady and her companion – for so they announced themselves – who had come down from Cheltenham: they spoke as though they had travelled from a distant tropical climatic zone to enjoy the healing *fraicheurs* of Devon.

Out of a context in which we had each learned to live with our secrets, my mother and I were paralysed by enforced public proximity. Later, she told me, she had intended to talk to me about the identity of my father, and to release me from the illusion that if the occasional occupant of the 'spare bedroom' was related to us, he was only so by marriage.

But she remained silent. I was twenty, and she perhaps judged me too immature to absorb such knowledge; and in any case, it was my last year at university, so perhaps she didn't want to disturb my pedagogic wanderings with Dante and Proust. And I certainly had no intention of telling her my secret, the unavowable aberration of my sexuality, outlawed at that time, the object of a taboo even more dreadful than that which surrounded her husband's disease; since by means of an arduous regime of medication at least *that* malady could be cured.

How could such an outing have been anything but a calamity? I remember it as overflowing with the choked *ennui* of the unspoken. The sun-bleached streets of Paignton, somnolent and deserted in the long afternoons of late August, only reflected the emptiness of the time that had to be got through, as though it were an alien element; as indeed it was, because we were both living elsewhere, she in her guilt-stained past, with the errant husband's sexual needs she had been unable to fulfil, and I in a distant future, where I would surely have met the man who was to transform my life; even though I had no idea how this was to be achieved.

I went for long walks on my own. Actually, they were not walks, but searches, voyages of exploration. I looked full into the face of every male between the ages of about eighteen and forty, a mute interrogation as to whether he were the one destined to relieve me of this oppressive loneliness, the sense of my unique strangeness and depravity. For that was how I thought of it. Since I had never disclosed to anyone the shaming secret of what I understood as my deviancy, I had no way of knowing that it was less particular than I imagined. Later, it appeared that eight or ten of our peers in the sixth form were gay; but in that time of straitened provincial tenseness, we never got round to sharing such confidences with one another.

So off I went, round the flowerbeds, the orange-and-lemon marigolds and silvery leaves of artemisia, purple petunias and the ubiquitous geraniums, along the cliff, with my copy of *The Complete Dante*, bound in red. I walked so far I exhausted myself, and then sat on the grass looking at the sea, which I detested for its repetitiveness: the waves that broke pointlessly on the sand, and then sucked the bladderwrack and ice-cream papers into the mouth of the sea, the clash of pebbles as they were stirred by the retreating waves, the silvery corrugation of the surface, the sun that struck live fluid sparks from the water – everything irritated me; but nothing more than the slow passage of the hours between breakfast and lunch, lunch and evening meal, and the luminous evenings that refused to fade. Many years later, when she was in a nursing home, and shortly before she died, my mother said to me, 'I hate every minute of it'; and I recognised exactly what she meant, because I have often felt the same, never more so than in the genteel cage of our penitential holiday together.

One day, I went out early and occupied a small grassy promontory on the cliff. It was a clear morning, with only the sound of the gulls on the wind, and I felt a melancholy relief that my mother had fallen in with the military man and his wife. I could only imagine that boredom had brought them together; although later, when I joined them, I was astonished to discover that they had discussed religion and found themselves united by a common unbelief.

My solitude was interrupted by the arrival of a stranger, who calmly sat down beside me on the little piece of ground overlooking the sea. He said nothing, but after a few minutes began to undress. He piled his clothes neatly beside him until he had stripped down to a pair of red swimming trunks. He then lay down in the sun and closed his eyes. He was about twenty-seven, lean, with tattoos on both arms. One said Mother, and on the other was a picture of a tombstone in red and blue. In place of the name of the occupant of the grave was written in blue ink R.I.P. LOVE.

There was no one nearby. Why had he chosen this particular spot? Had I usurped his customary place, and was he willing me to depart? I opened my Dante and pretended to concentrate on some particularly impenetrable verses from *Purgatorio*. My eyes kept stealing from the page to the body that was scarcely a foot from where I sat, smooth slightly sunburnt skin, fair body hair iridescent as the breeze moved it in the sun. He laced his hands behind his head, the mobile ellipse of his muscles contracted, and I could smell the faintly feral odour from the tangle of hair in the armpit. I stole a glance at the red tumulus of his genitals, which from time to time he stroked tenderly. I assumed he was as unaware of my presence as I was conscious of his. From the vulnerable whorl of the navel, a herringbone of hair darted to the edge of his trunks, which were taut over the hips, so that a slight aperture of dark shadow stood between the tight fabric and the lean protuberance of bone. Disturbed but transfixed, I could neither address him nor leave. He exuded such an air of containment I could not believe he noticed me at all. What enviable confidence in his right to exist in youthful splendour, lying with such naked negligence on the dry salty grass – I could not have imagined any such public abandon, nor any display of my body which I had never exposed to the sun and wind, and certainly not with pride and assurance, as he did now.

I could not think that, in spite of the considerable space around us, he should have chosen to lie so close to me, a taunt and an empty temptation, since I did not dare even to address a word to him. I did not move, and neither did he. The sun inscribed its burning arc on the sky, sank lower on the sea, an orange marigold on a silver stalk; and still I waited, thinking he might begin some trivial conversation, although I also knew that the moment to initiate communication was already long past. How familiar he had become in the few hours we had remained in the same place, I not reading Dante and he pretending to sleep, although I am sure he was conscious all the time; but I told myself he had come solely for the sun, to deepen the red-brown glow of his skin, the faint flaking of his scorched face.

I waited for him to go, which he did just before dark. He rose, stretched, all the while displaying his straight thorax and the corrugations of his rib-cage, the shifting mound of his sex, the cascade of hair that fell over his eyes as he stood up. He stepped into his trousers, tugged the short-sleeved green shirt over his head, slipped his feet into the sandals he had not even unbuckled, and disappeared down the slope towards the road, without so much as a glance in my direction.

How bereft I felt when he had gone, a premonition of loss of something I had never enjoyed. I remained a few minutes. The breeze was cool and the indigo water retained a faint stain of daylight that had almost vanished from the sky. How savourless everything seemed afterwards, the prospect of thinly spread bread and butter cut into triangles, the rock-cakes with their hard black currants, weak tea and the slice of pink meat. And my mother, worried sick about what had become of me, and I unable to tell her, because the nothing she had predicted had become of me.

He didn't return to the spot, although I did, the next day, and the next. Only five days of the holiday had elapsed, and even my mother, accustomed to my silences and withdrawals, noticed that I was more despondent than I had ever been.

I thought of the boy who had approached me in Rome. I had to understand that if I wanted anything, I would have to pay for it. My attractions were so meagre that there had to be some compensation for anyone who bestowed his company upon me.

In those two or three days, I wrote an essay on Dante, a copy of which remains with me after all these years, since, of all the callow productivity of my years at university, this one alone is associated with the mood of that long, eventful but unfulfilling summer. An aunt had recently given me a type-writer, a scratchy metal portable, with a ribbon half-black, half-red, which jumped each time a key was struck so that the text appeared in two colours on the page. It was about the Beatific Vision at the end of *Paradiso*, and it was almost certainly stained by my experience. It looks now extremely pretentious, but what I wrote was prompted by my own solitary exaltations.

At the end of the first week, my mother looked at me and said, 'Do you want to go home?' I could have wept with relief. We departed on the Monday, making an excuse about a sickness in the family – a truth we imagined to be falsehood. What a comfort it was to follow our separate paths, where we could be alone with the heavy secrets that had lain between us like lead while we were away from home.

I never again went away with my mother, although she did come to stay with me and my partner in London from time to time many years later. She disclosed to me and my brother the identity of our biological father when we were almost forty; I never came out to her as gay. There was no need to do so, since she simply accepted my relationship with my partner. He was with her when she died. I was in India.

I don't know if secrets like those which stood between my mother and me still impede expression of feelings between adults and their young. I would like to think they don't, since the constraint between us seriously impaired whatever benefits we might otherwise have derived from our close consanguinity and deep affection. We were both passionate in our way, but emotional communication between us was blocked by shame and guilt, and we never said to one another things we would surely have been thankful to utter in a less harshly puritanical time; but in such a time, these would almost certainly not have been secrets ...

ഇ ൙

After graduation Janet remained in Cambridge to study Arabic; but she never regained the poise and assurance of her early days. Her hands occasionally appeared to make small involuntary movements, a tremor when she lifted things. No one who had not known her before would have noticed it; but it was mortifying to Janet, since it struck deeply at the self she had crafted out of the overweight romantic young girl who had prayed for beauty among the Madonna lilies. Soumit, the friend from Delhi, had been seriously damaged in the punting accident. It had been, she remembered, a fine afternoon in summer, when he and some friends were idling on the river. He had slipped and missed his footing. It looked like a joke; only he had got caught up in some rope, and when his head failed to appear above the calm water, his friends jumped in, and dragged him to the sunny bank. He did not die but was badly injured and traumatised by the event. His parents had come from India but refused to meet Janet. His father was a high government official, and it was unthinkable they would acknowledge what they saw as casual dalliance, an unauthorised relationship with a foreign woman, when he had been destined for a union which would consolidate the landowning holdings of two influential families. Janet gave up her studies and went to work in the offices of a Japanese news agency in London.

It seemed that the already fragile bonds that had held Michael, Janet and me in their tenuous hold would be definitively broken when we left Cambridge. None of us then knew the importance we would have for each other for the rest of our lives.

Michael went to the United States. He had 'made a relationship', as he dramatically and creatively described it, with Victor, an anthropologist from a well-to-do liberal family in New Mexico. I am not sure that the phrase is accurate, since Michael's relationships were rarely seaworthy vessels. But he went off to America with great *éclat*; a leave-taking that was final, since he vowed never again to set foot in the snobbish class-ridden, country that had borne (and, he said, bored) him. He was good at disappearances. He also proved equally impressive in his ability to pop up unexpectedly at moments when it seemed he was in danger of being forgotten.

⃏ ℣

Victor was an erudite young man, attractive, of radical instincts. I still have a copy of a book he lent me, or rather gave, because it was never returned. This was Ruth Benedict's *Patterns of Culture*, which relativised the pretensions of the West in relation to allegedly more 'primitive' cultures. Every time I open it, I have reason to be grateful to Victor, since this was one of those rare influences that define for the reader things that she or he has obscurely felt but struggled to express.

Victor's parents were academics, and they welcomed Michael warmly. He basked in his own exoticism for as long as he could sustain it. But familiarity is the greatest enemy of the exotic qualities of others; and Michael's capacity to do nothing, to sleep until mid-afternoon and then wait for drinks to be served on the topaz tiles of the swimming-pool somewhat disappointed his hosts, who had, perhaps, anticipated greater intellectual stimulus than they received. Michael's monologue about the English Midlands proved less entertaining in that land of stories than he had imagined. His accounts of the rigours of the grinding poverty to which he had been schooled, were at odds with the ease to which he became so swiftly accustomed in the land of plenty. After a few months they suggested he might like to think about some form of employment.

They arranged work for him at the University of Illinois in Champaign-Urbana; at a remove from New Mexico which might suggest something of the emotional distance that had grown between the *enfant terrible* of the English working class and those who had offered him asylum from the misery of his origins.

Michael was immensely popular in the Midwest. He was novel, entertaining, irreverent. Most of his students were young women, and he was invited to many of their homes, where not a few saw in him a possible future husband. This did not displease Michael, because he was never in the slightest danger of losing his heart to any of them, that rock-like organ petrified by early maternal rejection.

He communicated once to his mother. Sitting in the Sociology department office of the University of Illinois, he made a recording which he sent to her for Christmas. He invented what he thought she would like America to be. It went, 'Hello Mom. It is snowing hard here and the temperature is twenty degrees below freezing. I have a car, because you have to travel 80 miles just to do your shopping. I went to four Thanksgiving parties. For my lunch I just had a duck hamburger and corn-on-the cob. I am going to stay with a very rich family for Christmas. They have a ranch and a few thousand acres. Well, the tape is running out, so Happy Christmas. I hope you like the electric carving knife I sent. See you some day soon.'

But he didn't. No one heard from him for more than a year. Later, he returned with multiple versions of his career in the USA. He had joined an underground revolutionary cell, had been denounced and served time in prison. He had fathered several children and run away from each woman. He had helped form a trade union among down-and-outs. He had become an alcoholic and lived in a hospital. He got into a fight in a saloon and bit off his opponent's ear. He had been gambling, whoring and agitating in the stockyards of Chicago. Many of his narratives sounded oddly similar to the movie versions of America on which we had been raised. It was impossible to discover what had really happened during the missing year in his life.

One day his parents arrived at our house in a state of great agitation. My mother invited them in and Mrs O'Neill broke down in tears. 'Has Jerry heard anything from Michael?' 'Not for months.' 'He's not at the address he gave us.' Mrs O'Neill had read in the paper how, when the spring thaws come to the Midwest, many bodies are discovered, preserved by the months of frost in which they had perished. 'Do you think that could have happened to Michael?' she whispered, almost afraid to utter the words, because speaking them might make them come true. I was about to laugh scornfully, but my mother's look quenched my reaction. She said, 'Why don't you ask at the American Embassy? They must have a record of anything that's happened to him.' She gave them coffee with a strong brandy, and Mr O'Neill said he would go to the Embassy on his first free day.

℘ ℘

After Cambridge I went home to Northampton. I did not return in the style in which I had arrived, but caught the

128 United Counties bus, which went to Northampton via Bedford, a slow and uncomfortable conveyance, in which the slight changes of accent between the villages could be heard as the bus proceeded through the small towns and villages of East Anglia into the Midlands. This was not the homecoming I had anticipated. There was no welcoming party. I simply walked into the living room, where my mother and aunt urged on the finalists of the world snooker championship, in a programme called *Pot Black*.

I knew I would have to work, and the most congenial labour seemed to be in the public library, where I was immediately offered a post. No one asked me to account for this spectacular example of downward mobility. If this was viewed by my mother as a failure of mine, it was a slightly bitter triumph for her, for her prophecies had been fulfilled. I would never amount to much.

The not much that I would amount to was verified by my first pay slip, which was for £7 10 shillings. 'After three years at the most famous university in the world,' said Uncle Arthur contemptuously, 'you'd have got more if you'd gone to sweep the roads.' He was persuaded that higher education was the gateway to a life of misery (an observation with which I did not, for once, disagree with him), and he thanked God he at least had been spared such a fate.

The shame of going back to Northampton was not to be borne. Michael was in America, Janet was learning Arabic, while I was stamping love-books for Councillor Mrs Collins. She would come in with an armful of volumes, throw them on the counter and say, 'Get me eight more like those.' I once tried to explain to her the difference between a public and a private servant; whereupon she lost her temper and, flushing scarlet, through clenched teeth, said, 'This will cost you your job.' She demanded to see the Chief Librarian, who, immediately summoned from his room, assured her the matter would be dealt with. He would not tolerate insubordination or rudeness in his staff. Mollified, but still muttering about 'jumped-up cheese-counter assistants', she walked with dignity out of the library, leaving behind her copies of *'Neath What Dark Skies?* and *On What Distant Shore?*. The librarian grinned at me. He said, 'Take no notice of her.' She was well known to the staff. They called her Fanny by Gaslight.

Going home after Cambridge was perceived more widely than I could have imagined as a humiliation. 'Back again, are you?' people asked; while some of my teachers were shocked. They felt they had launched me into the world, on a luxury liner, and I had reappeared on a broken-down fishing-boat.

It was known in that discerning town that too much book-learning unbalanced you; and some people looked at me sympathetically, assuming that I must have had a 'nervous breakdown', an affliction to which, it was widely believed, both women and intellectuals were prey. I was trapped. I could not walk in the sunny main street without seeing three or four people I knew; and I dreaded their scorn, which was sometimes indistinguishable from their sympathy.

It would not do for me to skulk around the site of my shame, inventing reasons for my reappearance in a place from which I was to have shaken the dust off my feet forever. Here I was a revenant from what was supposed to be a superior afterlife. Stephen, a school friend, had gone to Paris and found work on the strength of nothing more than an ability to speak English; this accomplishment was unproblematic then, since any native speaker was automatically qualified to transmit the tongue, without too much in the way of pedagogic theory.

So another ceremonial leave-taking occurred. My return to Northampton had been nothing but an interlude, a vacation, while I decided what to do with my life. This very idea was an extraordinary innovation, because most people had previously never 'done anything' with their lives. Life had happened to them; and their destiny was inscribed in the very structures of the town – from the maternity hospital to the red-brick school, from the boot factories to the football ground, from the chapel to the pub, and from the geriatric ward to the cemetery. Whatever consolations I found in the familiar landscapes of home, permanent residence was still not to be one of them.

శ్రం ఇర్

I wrote to Stephen, who said there would be no problem finding work. He met me at the Gare du Nord, after a terrifying journey which had involved taking the 'milk-train' to London at 4.30 in the morning, in order to catch the 'boat-train' and make the connection in Calais. Stephen was staying in Buzenval, a working-class suburb, and living in a hostel for students from French overseas territories. Bed was just a mattress on the floor. Would that be OK? he asked. Having encountered a number of people from former imperial territories, I supposed that would be all right. But nothing prepared me for the disturbing, erotic interlude I was about to experience. I slept on a paillasse among scores of young men, the very existence of whose countries roused only a faint echo of distant geography lessons. I was too much in awe of them even to think of offering them my services as teacher; since I could imagine no earthly language in which I could address them. I lingered in the hostel, dazzled by the splendid bodies of a Tunisian boy called Mahfouz and a Senegalese student with the – to me androgynous – name, Patrice. I watched them undress through a hole I had made in the coarse blanket, thrilled by the silky darkness of Patrice's legs, and the honeyed knots of Mahfouz' spine as he bent to remove his jeans. It was summer. The hostel was overcrowded and the night penetrated by the peppery scent of youth and the melodic murmur of its dreams. Patrice and Mahfouz spoke in a thrilling French; their accent suggested revolution, passion and causes from which we had been shielded; and they filled me with a wild longing to join them in projects which made of Marx's prophecies sombre dreams worth dying for, even if I secretly felt them unrealisable. I went to the theatre with a young man from Gabon called Emile (like Rousseau I asked, but he had never heard of Rousseau). We saw a play by Eugene Ionesco called *Les Chaises*, about an orator who comes to give his message of salvation to an excited throng of people; but when he opens his mouth, only a few disjointed words come out. I imagined a future for myself in Gabon, although I never defined the role I might play in that country. Certainly Emile – whose father had the romantic occupation of dealer in traditional non-timber products of the rainforest – had no intention of returning. I bought Emile a watch and some clothes with my fast-diminishing resources. He wondered why I was staying in the hostel if I was so rich. I said it was to meet people like him. He showed little enthusiasm and soon detached himself from my company. My meagre store of money wasted, my efforts at finding work were half-hearted, so I went back, ignominiously, once more to Northampton.

୫୦ ଓଃ

This time, I had an excuse. I applied for a job as teacher in one of the poorest schools in town but was found to have a shadow on my lung. I was relieved; not only because it would exempt me for a time from having to face a class of recalcitrant thirteen-year-olds, but also because, well instructed in literature, I knew something of the tradition of tragic consumptives. I sat in the back garden, under the pear-tree, with its scaly bark and wizened fruit which never ripened, and which even my thrifty mother ceased gathering because they were fit for nothing but the wasps, which drowned in the pulpy juice as they rotted on the grass. She watched me through the dusty window pane as she sat in her chair, a chair from which she would soon fear to get up as she became housebound with agoraphobia; and I would go in to find her weeping. 'It's such a waste,' she said. 'I watch you sitting there, and all I want is for you to find a nice girl to settle down with.' She fed me with an egg beaten up in sherry every morning. Reproachfully tender, her every gesture was a reproof that I had wilfully spoilt the good health she had carefully nurtured, and that I had not given her grandchildren.

Neither yet, had my brother. His life and mine diverged dramatically when I went to the grammar school while he was relegated to the bottom class of what was then called a 'secondary modern' school – bearing in its name its subordinate status and a false ring of contemporary relevance. We grew up as strangers to each other, partly because we were temperamentally antagonistic, but also because this separation suited our mother: perhaps she was frightened that we might combine against her. Her experience of men suggested that she expected no great rewards from her sons. Later, my brother became far more successful than I was: a skilled craftsman, he became a restorer of historic buildings in Devon; and he developed an early contempt for the abstract worlds in which I and my friends loitered. He died fifteen years ago from mesothelioma, an asbestos-related cancer, as a result of his early work constructing car-parks in Zambia and South Africa. The estrangement between us never healed.

🙲 🙳

After a few months spent preparing for an even more definitive farewell to Northampton than my trips to Cambridge or Paris, I was declared fit to take up my post; and in a vain tribute to the brother I had scorned, I taught for two years in what was then regarded as the poorest secondary school in Northampton. I was unsuited to the role; although I did help one or two boys consigned to the sluggish currents of the C-stream to overcome the assumption that they were ineducable; and one boy in particular, who had never learned to read or write, became marvellously proficient under my tutelage. In that dark age, it was still customary to beat children for bad behaviour; in this place of learning, by means of a plimsoll (a forerunner of trainers) applied to the backside. As punishment it was extremely ineffective, unless the master applied great force. A boy guilty of some misdemeanour would be told to bend over – which he invariably did – to receive the blow with the rubber sole of the footwear. Afterwards, he would mutter a defiant, 'Didn't hurt,' and return to his place. This was known at the time as 'discipline', without which, it was feared, the lower classes (in both a social and pedagogic sense) would cease to know their place. Because I could not maintain order, I was regarded by the staff as a passenger; and the senior English teacher – a stocky Scot whose mastery of the language he was teaching was not impressive – would burst into my room, brandishing a cane and demanding to know why we were making such a racket. It was, I explained, a drama lesson. He said if they didn't keep quiet, he'd administer enough drama to last them a lifetime. I fretted over my inability to keep order, since some teachers seemed to regard their principal task as a supplement to that of the police force.

Although I had become a teacher, with status, salary and respectability, at home I remained in a condition of subservience. I was like those countries which at that time were declaring independence from Empire without freeing themselves from the social, cultural and economic supremacy of their former masters. My mother claimed a right of access to every aspect of my life. This was, to some degree, a survival of an archaic view of kinship: the lives of family members were not independent entities, but formed part of a shared existence, in which individuals were protectors and custodians of everybody else.

It felt nothing like that when my mother exercised her 'right' to intercept my letters and read them. One day I had answered an advertisement in the *New Statesman*, in which a man was searching for a companion for holidays and leisure. At that time, this was code for gay contacts. I had made an arrangement to meet the man outside Knightsbridge Tube Station. It was a chill November evening. He was a pleasant and quite attractive individual, and he suggested we go for a walk in Hyde Park. Although slightly surprised by the proposal of such a cheerless outing, I agreed. When we had walked a few hundred metres into the park, he stopped and said, 'Now show me your cock.' I was appalled and fled. Apparently undeterred by my prudishness, he wrote me a passionately explicit letter.

I arrived home from work at the library to find my mother silent with suppressed rage. 'What's the matter?' I asked anxiously. 'What's the matter?' she echoed, 'this is what's the matter.' She flourished the open letter in fury. 'What's this? What does it mean?' Her voice rose to a shriek. 'Is it men that you want? Is that it? Is it men you want?' 'No Mum, of course not,' I said weakly. It didn't occur to me to question her right to tamper with my correspondence. I felt myself unmasked. I was led to believe that all hopes for the wealth, success and happy family future for which my mother had suffered untold deprivations, lay in ruins.

❧ ☙

Soon after this Michael came home. His mother and father had traced him through the Foreign Office. He was on the point of being deported anyway, for no more subversive a reason than that his visa had expired, and he had neglected to renew it. This was how the myth evolved of his life as a fugitive in

America. His parents sent the air fare. And one day, there he was, a man transformed, full of mystery, with just enough of an accent to let us know where he had been. He knocked on our door; I even recognised the knock. He said pleasantly, 'Hello Mrs Seabrook.' She said, 'Where the bloody hell have you been? We were expecting you for your tea. That was three years ago.'

Michael said, 'I went to America.' My mother held up her hand. 'I shan't ask what you've been doing. Only one thing I know, you've broke your mother's heart.' Then, 'What have you been doing?'

'You know. Meeting people.'

'Damn long way to go to meet people isn't it? Aren't there enough of them here.'

After she had left us alone in the parlour, I said to Michael, 'I suppose Northampton must seem a bit pathetic to you now.'

'It is, a bit. I think I can bear it for the weekend. Just about.'

'Oh Michael, have some compassion for those who have to spend their whole lives here. Like your parents.'

'They have no choice. Those I pity are people who could get out and don't.'

'Michael, your horizons are so wide. I wonder the world is big enough for you.'

'Well there's only one place I could live in this country now, and that's London.'

'Don't get lost there, will you Michael? What's happened to your voice?'

'Nothing. It's broken I expect.'

'Well they've set it very badly. You sound like Doris Day.'

'All right. See you around. I hope you're still drinking your hot milk at night. You must come up to London some time. If the journey isn't too arduous.'

'Thanks for the invitation Michael. I'll bring Sheila.'

'Who's Sheila?'

I hadn't told Michael I was engaged. I sensed it was a mistake, but I had not yet admitted — confessed — acknowledged — to myself that I was gay. My attraction to men existed in another sphere from that in which I imagined I would do my mother's bidding, which she described as 'settling down'. I thought that the word 'homosexuality' referred solely to sexual acts; and it never occurred to me that love relationships between members of the same sex might be possible; a belief reinforced by my experience with Michael. I still cherished the idea that a future wife might arouse in me all the attributes claimed by the cultural cliches of the time for 'love'. Our capacity to hide from ourselves is, it seems, unlimited. If we dissimulate before others, this is nothing compared to our ability to deceive ourselves, especially those of our multiple selves we do not want the world to see.

Michael was nonplussed; which pleased me. He said, 'That's nice. I expect you'll want a present. I'll buy you a nice poker-work motto to hang over your bed. Abandon all hope all who enter here.' He said, 'Can I come to the wedding?'

'No, as a matter of fact. It's going to be quiet.'

'Like the grave.' He lingered. 'Oh well, I suppose I'd better be off. Lone and friendless as usual. So long.'

'How long Michael?'

'So bloody long, you won't believe it.'

My mother came back into the room while he was still thinking of some even more cutting valedictory words. 'Jerry.' She was excited. 'There's a lovely little terraced house going round the corner in Alexandra Road. You shan't want for linen. I've got some beautiful pillow-slips embroidered by your Great-Aunt Li before she went blind. They've never been used since they were on old Granny Timms' death-bed.'

Michael ran away as fast as his long-distance runner's legs could carry him. He later said he felt he had just been to my funeral.

ℰꙮ ᏳᏚ

He found a semi-derelict flat in a Peabody Building close to Holborn. Employment was even easier to come by. He worked in an ice-lolly factory in Acton, a form of manufacturing undreamed of in the days when people knew a good bit of Northampton shoe leather when they saw it. The workers had to wear specially hygienic boots, because a lot of the liquid spilled from the vats onto the floor, and this was swept up and returned to the production line. He said it cured him in advance of any taste he might have developed for that particular form of confectionery.

The flat was without basic amenities. On his third day there, Janet arrived. 'Darling Michael, I've come to stay with you.' Janet was already suffering from the effects of the undiagnosed multiple sclerosis, which had already diminished her life. She brought all her worldly possessions, a saucepan, a Japanese parasol and an ivory fan. 'I'll have the bedroom and you can sleep in the kitchen. Isn't the room ghastly? Never mind, I'll do some murals. That horrid damp patch reminds me of Europa and the Bull.' She set to work, extemporising on the stain, which was duly incorporated into her collage of images from Greek and Roman mythology. The antipathy between Michael and Janet remained unspoken, and only came to the surface in their conflicting friendship with me. A shared distaste for the home town and the experience of going through university together created a bond between us, and indeed linked together for a time the lives of Janet and Michael, who would only later discover how little they actually liked each other.

Michael and Janet lived a chaotic improvised existence. There was no sink, so they did the washing up in a cardboard box. This had to be renewed every two or three days because it was soon reduced to pulp. When Mr and Mrs O'Neill visited, feeling vindicated that their son had returned to the capital, they were anxious to see how well Michael had done for himself. His mother wept because it reminded her of her orphaned years in Little Dorrit Buildings. Janet offered them tripe and onions, because she thought this a suitable working-class fare. 'No thank you,' Mrs O'Neill shuddered. When she sat on the dingy sofa, she was alarmed to find a pile of bones underneath. 'What's this? A skeleton?' Janet was apologetic. 'No it's only bones. I was going to make some soup. Only I forgot.'

Michael, despite forsaking Northampton forever, was a frequent visitor. We took up our friendship almost as though he had never been away. Neither of us had ever been as comfortable with anyone else as we were in each other's company. He asked, 'How's your engagement Jerry?' I said 'Long. How is Janet?' 'The same. A bit more so maybe.'

Then there was another period of silence from Michael. He had met Alastair, and was planning to move into his house.

Alastair had been brought up – fetched up, he called it – in a Barnardo's institution near Kircudbright. He had never known his parents, but had been told that his father was a hospital consultant and his mother a nurse; so it was not difficult to piece together the nature of the relationship that had produced him and declared him, in a fit of bureaucratic compassion, 'an orphan'. His institutional life – of discipline, order, prosaic literalness and lack of love – had scarred him deeply, though perhaps less so than his first experience of the outside world. He had gone to the army recruitment centre in a neighbouring town just after his fifteenth birthday, this being the occasion when charity children were believed to be able to stand on their own feet and take the burden of their living costs off the state or whichever philanthropic institution had taken them in. The recruiting officer had told him to strip; and when he had done so, he was pushed to the floor and raped. Since he had been raised to have faith in whatever adults in authority told him, he suffered this humiliation in silence, and told no one at the home what had happened. It was only many years later that he was able to assess the effects of the violence done to him.

At the time, it only added to the burden of repression in which the institution had already instructed him. He was obsessively tidy, deferential and punctilious, dutiful and intolerant of other people, unless they were gay.

He had met Michael in that – for gay people at the time – most common, if uncongenial, of places where acquaintances were made; the urinal at the bottom of Dog Kennel Hill in South London. This was, after all, the early 1960s, before the hour of enlightenment had struck. Neither Michael nor Alastair was under any illusion about the nature of the relationship. Neither wanted anything to do with what they called slushy sentimentality. Alastair was brusque and emphatic, while Michael was well steeled against involvements that might demand any dredging of the night-dark depths of feeling. Both were, as it were, experts in emotional surgery: proficient in by-passing the heart.

They rented a flat in Hammersmith, a newly built structure in silver-grey brick, with wide windows which rattled fiercely as District Line trains sped by within a few feet. There were multiple advantages in the apartment – it was compact, easy to clean, close to the shops, convenient for transport. There was only one serious drawback in the arrangements, and that was the length of time Michael would have to spend in the hours between work and sex. He was by this time teaching in a secondary school, and Alastair's duties allowed him to reach home before five o'clock. Long, possibly savourless, stretches of time lay before him. Michael required entertainment, of a kind scarcely to be fulfilled by the limited number of TV channels in Britain at that time and their almost indistinguishable programmes. It was, therefore, natural that he should think of me in this role, knowing, as he did, that I was languishing in Northampton, between waiting for the end of the term when the man from the Band of Hope came to address school-leavers on the evils of drink, with the visual aid of a pickled human liver as supporting evidence, and going to see Adam Faith perform at the Savoy cinema with friends I had made during my sojourn in the library.

The idea of sharing a flat with Michael and Alastair came like a promise of deliverance. My engagement was not formally broken off: it dissolved in a mutual recognition of the delusion it had been. I became more conscious of my sexuality, which appeared out of the mists of a prolonged adolescence like the contours of a continent I never knew existed. I felt both guilt and grief at my capacity for the deception I had practised, both on Sheila and on myself. I cannot say that I ever admitted that I was gay before this time: an obscure discomfort accompanied me but while it remained unarticulated, it remained in shadow, in the vague terrain between innocence and ignorance.

All this ought to have made me pause to wonder what I was doing when I agreed to share a flat with Michael and Alastair; I never asked myself where the obtuse angle might lie in this triangular piece of emotional geometry.

໖ ໖

I applied to the London School of Economics for a course in Social Administration. It had been axiomatic that education was the primary site for the reform and reconstruction of the working class; but teachers were unanimous that 'it' all began in the home; a monosyllable which covered such diverse social phenomena as bad manners, irresponsibility, insolence, idleness, lack of respect and all the unfamiliar characteristics of people being led out of industrial bondage. It was clearly the home one had to get into, in order to understand – and influence positively – the social transformation then taking place. And the only people who, at that time, had free passage into the homes of the people were social workers. A diploma in Social Administration was just the thing: it would earn me the right to practise, pending deeper instruction; but it would suffice as a kind of search-warrant to enter into the popular psyche in its strange, shifting shape, perhaps even to make sense of the mysterious churnings which the 1960s were producing there.

It should, of course, be remembered, that at that time, social workers were not yet regarded as idle functionaries or neglectful busybodies whose inattention to their duties made them responsible for parents eager to torture, maim or kill their children. It seemed then that, while the improvements in the lives of most people had been spectacular, certain laggards of affluence had been left behind; unable to adapt to the sudden good fortune which had swept the majority in a mass élan of upward mobility. The role of social workers was to facilitate the passage of recalcitrants – the former rough working class – into a world of easy consumption and a mood of industrialised euphoria, which had replaced the sombre trinity of work, want and woe.

Social workers were regarded – briefly, and as it appears now, incredibly – as secular saints. It was a profession at which people marvelled, wondering how anyone had the patience and commitment to linger on the fate of the feckless, the wastrels of the world. They would say, 'I think the work you do is marvellous. Of course, I couldn't do it myself, I'm too sensitive.' It was only later, when it became clear that the purpose of social workers was not to usher latecomers into the consumerist mainstream, but to featherbed and mollycoddle scroungers and spongers, to make excuses for the criminals they had become. Then, social workers became an object of public odium. By that time I had already fled the profession, perhaps in anticipation of the forces of hatred gathering on its borders.

I relished the opening created by a mixture of academic opportunity and the machinations of Michael; and, accordingly, bade yet another farewell to the weary watchers on the shore, who once more waved their no longer tear-stained handkerchiefs as the liner of liberty pulled away from the quay.

Although I had met Alastair several times and established a cool cordiality with him, it did not take long for me to realise the trap into which I had fallen: I was, apparently, one of the conditions upon which Michael had agreed to live with Alastair; and as such, I soon became the object of intense resentment which such abstractions are liable to provoke. Alastair's love of neatness and order became burdensome; and if I neglected any of the duties assigned to me, I was punished by a silence so profound and so cutting that it was almost like being thrashed. It devolved upon me – since I didn't have regular hours, and was, in any case, in that contemptible category of humanity, a student – to take and bring the washing from the launderette. I was then expected to iron every item, including underwear and socks. This hated chore was inspected by Alastair every Monday evening; and any item in which creases remained was separated from the rest and left on the sideboard, as admonition and reproach, to be ironed later, and properly, by Alastair.

When washing up, any piece of cutlery which found its way into the wrong compartment in the drawer was not quietly put back in its rightful place, but was left, accusingly, on top of the kitchen unit, that I might learn, not only the proper place for each fish-knife and fork, but also my own; which was, to Alastair, certainly not in this pseudo-family household, in which Alastair was the stern paterfamilias, I an indulgent and scatty mother, and Michael the wayward but spoilt child. This also set up a replica of the *ménage à trois* into which his father had stepped when Michael was six; only this time, he, and not the hero returned from the wars, was the only possible victor.

ℬ ℛ

There were still long vacant days of tedium, even though by this time concealment of our sexual orientation had long ago lapsed. We understood that although secretiveness and avoidance might have been a response to the punitive temper of the times when we were young, we had not yet openly acknowledged that these things had also bitten deeply into our relationship with each other.

One Good Friday morning Michael and I decided we would write a play. The material for it had been offered by the two young women who lived next door. They were smart Northern girls, who had come to London with the idea of breaking into show business; not on their own account, but with the assistance of the little girl, Lisa's child, who they intended to take to auditions to advertising companies. The father of this three-year-old, who came from a well-to-do family, had disappeared, it was believed, to marry someone of 'his own class'; but he had given Lisa two thousand pounds to bring up the baby. Lisa and her friend, Michelle, had instantly left Bolton for London, rented a flat, and besieged every advertising company they could find. Louella, the baby, was a delight. 'Everyone at home fell in love with her.' Michelle said, 'She's gonna break some hearts before long.' 'Yeh,' said her mother, 'mine's one of 'em.'

They had already made a TV advert for cough syrup for infants. Louella had shown a distinct talent for acting; and had played the part of a sick child with great conviction. They were now auditioning for a role in an advertisement for package holidays. The only problem was that Louella was too pale. 'That's all right,' said Lisa, 'we'll get a sun-lamp make her golden, and look like she's enjoying her holiday.' They had been as good as their word. They had observed strict instructions that they should on no account leave the child under the lamp for more than forty minutes a day. One afternoon, they had had a couple of drinks with some men friends, and had forgotten to retrieve Louella from the harmful effects of the lamp; they were alerted only when she started to scream. The poor little girl had not only become several shades too dark ('She looks like a bleeding Paki,' the distraught mother wailed), but her skin had blistered and she required medical treatment. Her career was ruined before she was four. Lisa and Michelle had been counting on the money from the next assignment, and they fled, leaving two or three months' unpaid rent.

To Michael and me this story appeared like a metaphor for working-class ambition, a guileless desire to rise in the world, which had been corrupted and spoilt by capitalist consumer society. Perhaps we also saw in it a parable of our own story of escape. We wrote the play over Easter. It was not very good, but we found we were skilled at dialogue, especially at reproducing a quick working-class wit. This play would be the forerunner of a considerable output; an occupational therapy for the *ennui* of Michael's relationship and for my lack of one.

We also had a gift for mimicking working-class women; and we fell into the roles effortlessly, acting out, not only the characters of our mothers, but also the conflict between us – the competitive struggle, the denial to each other of our sexuality, and an absence of expressed feeling. The plays, however dramatically deficient, were funny, since they combined a poignant authenticity of the life of the streets with the adroit perception and verbal fluency of women.

As a child, I had learned the wrong language: I had always expressed myself in the idiom of women, because this was more vivid and trenchant than the language men used. There had always been an informal gender apartheid in working-class communities, and this was reflected in the way people communicated (or often failed to do so). Working men were laconic, gruff and as sparing with words as they were with the insufficient cash in their pockets. Their speech consisted principally of commands to wives and children, together with a few observations on football and racing, and some obscenities reserved for foremen and bosses. After a few beers they might expound their dour view of the world; a conviction that poverty was a crime against the poor and nothing would change till you were put to bed with a shovel. But women had always been custodians of feeling and relationships, and the words that fell from their sharp tongues were always vibrant and more subtle than the didactic certainties of men.

Out of this mixture of suppressed emotion and cross-gendered linguistic fluency, the plays reflected a struggle between the quick-witted and incisive and the manipulative but easy-going. It was not that the characters represented one or the other of us: parts of both battled within each persona, and this gave our modest endeavours a certain dynamic energy. It was private therapy as public theatre.

We were given money by the Arts Council which permitted us to spend a year 'developing' our plays; but since our own development had been so stunted, there was no very impressive outcome. This privilege would be abridged by the asperities of Thatcherism and the absence of any further grant, with which the Arts Council had, apparently, been too wantonly liberal.

We had some faint public recognition. When one of our plays at the Royal Court, although directed by the brilliant Peter Gill, failed to attract an audience, the management declared it to be of sufficient social importance for tickets to be given away for nothing. The queues were extensive and the theatre full; but that put paid to any hope of commercial success.

❦ ❧

Our circumstances were about to change. Alastair had inherited a collection of postage stamps from a man in South Africa, an individual who had befriended him while he was in the Royal Navy and with whom he had lived for a few years. This stamp collection was worth several thousand pounds and, with the money from the sale, Alastair decided to buy a house in South London.

This was a rather imposing villa built in the 1880s, as the railway reached some of the remoter suburbs; a slightly ornate, if cramped, dwelling which had been preserved intact by its owner: there were scrolls of oak-leaves and acorns in the brick-work, a motif repeated along the cornices of what estate agents call 'reception' rooms; and although Alastair, with his austere taciturnity, was unlikely to do much receiving, he wanted to restore them to their high Victorian splendour. Each oak-leaf was painted green, and the acorns a deep maroon; the roses in the centre moulding were pink and their foliage a paler green. The walls were painted deep blue, with white lighting to illuminate the cut glass decanters and glasses which had been an ancillary part of the bequest. Our friends, many of whom visited only once, called it the South London gin palace.

This transformation took several months; and while it was being completed, Michael and I truanted from the tedium of doing our share by invoking our creative 'work'. The time was also lightened by frequent visits from Janet, for whom there was ample accommodation in the four bedrooms. She injudiciously criticised Alastair's taste, but she managed to do so in a way that seemed to him flattery. 'Darling,' she said, 'you've captured the essence of Victorian kitsch.'

ଛ ଓ

One day, Janet greeted me with the words, 'I am so relieved. I've found out I have multiple sclerosis.' The relief was because the disease that had been tormenting her had for so long defied diagnosis. That she could give a name to what was wrong was, at first, a great comfort: she no longer had to attribute it to characteristics she might have been expected to take responsibility for – clumsiness, carelessness, distractedness. For years it had remained obscure, the more frightening because unidentified, this curious gaucherie in a woman so elegant, the loss of balance in one so poised, the memory lapses in a mind that had been capable of absorbing a new language within weeks – she had swiftly acquired a competence in Arabic, Turkish and Urdu – had become a great source of shame, and an apparent betrayal of the promise everyone said she showed. The identifiable reason for her accelerating decline provided some consolation for her ebbing competences.

Actually, all Janet's greetings were sparkling and animated. On mornings when she had washed her hair in Girton, she would wrap her head in a towel and come into central Cambridge on her bicycle to dry it by my gas-fire; she spread it on the hearthrug, an iridescent fan of fine silk. She would burst into my bedroom, her presence, accompanied by the cool breath of morning, a reproach that I was wasting the best part of a beautiful autumn day. She often brought some delicacy – chestnut *purée* or patum peperium – which we ate out of the container, in defiance of gastronomic propriety. Her capacity for joy was irresistible. I hoped that her spontaneous enthusiasm might be contagious and wanted her to show me how to be happy. Human sensibilities, however, resemble tickets for airlines or libraries, in that they are not transferable.

Her happiness was never feigned or thoughtless. She saw the best in everybody, even when it was absent; and remarkably, few people failed to live up to her hopeful, if unfashionable, expectations. In the early days of her decline, she lived in squalid surroundings. She was determined to remain independent of her parents, and succeeded in concealing from them the extent of her growing disability. For two years she lived up a cork-screw staircase of a Pakistani greengrocery in Hackney, where she had to pick her way through crates of mildewed oranges, decaying coriander and onions that had sprouted in the damp. The rent was negligible, since she looked after the premises when the owners went back to Pakistan for extended periods. There, she learned Punjabi and played with the children. She always sought to transcend the most depressing environment, looking through the skylight smeared with birdshit and pleased at her good fortune in being able to see the sky, and befriending the elderly men who sat in Victoria Park, one of whom told her she was the spitting image of Theda Bara.

Janet never concealed her emotional entanglements. The man with whom she had the most tempestuous but most enduring relationship was Caleb, from Sierra Leone. Caleb was violent and abusive, and Janet, who advocated absolute freedom of thought and feelings, acknowledged her emotional – and physical – submission to a man so obsessively jealous that when he went to work, he would lock her in his flat without any clothes, so that she would not be tempted to break out. She was not allowed to meet any of her friends, even those of us who were gay, for whom, in any case Caleb had the greatest contempt, since he knew that, as sinners, we were doomed to eternal fires. If they were in a restaurant, he would suddenly exclaim, 'Why are you looking at that man?' overturning the table as he dragged her away from the uneaten meal. 'Why did that woman smile at you?' 'Who do you see when I am away?' He would examine the windows to see whether the sash had been disturbed during his absence. Janet was never frightened by these displays; and answered any questions about the inconsistencies between behaviour and feminist views with a shrug, saying *le coeur a ses raisons ...*. She said she needed the discipline of Caleb's exigent attachment to preserve her from emotional chaos.

And possibly also, from anxiety over the mysterious erosion within. She had been to hospitals that specialised in tropical diseases, with neurological disorders, and even, shamingly, clinics which could trace rare forms of sexually transmitted disorders. She spent years awaiting the results of tests, swabs, biopsies, tissue cultures, with no conclusive result. Her Christian heritage whispered retribution for sin; and although she had in theory dismissed what she saw as superstition, the figure of her father, whom she loved dearly, still loomed spectrally over her unbelief.

She was staying with us one weekend, after the illness had been diagnosed, and she had become unsteady on her feet. She received a call from a former boy-friend in Nigeria. He was coming to London for a few days, and wanted her to stay with him in his hotel. He was now a member of the Nigerian government who had grown rich in the oil boom. He had booked a double room at the Hilton hotel in Park Lane. Would Janet please be there on a certain Friday afternoon. She explained that she was no longer the woman he had known, that she had a degenerative disease which restricted her movements and inhibited her socially. He dismissed her objections, and told her to dress up, since they would be going to this fashionable restaurant, a casino and, because he knew Janet loved it, the opera, to see *Nabucco*. They went shopping at Asprey's in Bond Street and then he invited her to choose an evening dress, something so far from her thoughts and daily life that she laughed aloud. But the luxury and the sexual excitement suggested a future for her. When he spoke of corruption in his country, he did so with approval, which discouraged Janet from enquiring into the extravagances she was enjoying. She understood that this might be the first of many such occasions; and she returned to our modest hospitality as though life would never be the same again.

But no further calls came from Nigeria. She sat by the telephone, weekend after weekend, her face shiny with tears, as she tried to contact his office in Lagos. He was always 'in a meeting' or 'out of the country'. She was once put through to a woman who demanded, in an uxorious tone, who was speaking. For several weeks Janet continued to hope that this had not been a simple interlude in her decline; but with time, came to accept that this had, indeed, been an exceptional moment. 'How could I have been so deluded?' A little later, she said with resignation 'Well that's that, I suppose.' Actually it wasn't. Among the debris of what she saw as her wasted life (not in the sense of squandered, but atrophied), other compensatory experiences lay in store.

Michael and I wrote many plays for radio. They followed a formulaic structure, but the dialogue, irreverent and funny, captivated certain BBC personnel, who thought them a rare excursion into a social realism not always prominent in their schedules. On what was then still known as the Third Programme – words which came to be associated with the highbrow and the avant-garde – we were proud to hear the solemn tones of the announcer introduce *Once Round Lill, Twice Round the Gasworks*; and we were sure we detected a note of disdain in his over-punctilious voice. The play was set on a South London estate, one of those brick four-storey blocks from the 1920s, built around an echoing courtyard, where people hung out their washing, children played and teenagers made a nuisance of themselves. Life spilt out onto the balconies and into the courtyards; it was a semi-public spectacle. Bingo Lill, overweight and waddling, wears bandages round her legs 'for sympathy', and her breath smells like a gas-leak; she lives next door to Kath, razor-tongued, thin as a whippet and twice as fast. Lill's youngest son, Gary, refuses to go to school, thieves everything that moves in the block, lights fires because he loves to see things burn; and takes his grubby dog with him everywhere on a piece of string, even sleeping with it in bed.

We played out the roles, changing from one to the other spontaneously. We both had characteristics of each: Michael was Lill because he was self-indulgent, liked an easy life; and I was Lill because I never challenged anything. Michael was Kath in that he always had his eye on the main chance; and I was Kath because I was clear-sighted enough to foresee the consequences of things.

The dialogue went:

Lill: 'Ere, Kath.

KATH: Lill, what's the matter? You look white as a sheet, not one of yours of course.

LILL: No Kath. It's me book. It's gone.

KATH: What book? Bleeding liar Lill, you know you can't read.

LILL: No. Me Assistance Book. Two weeks' money gone wiv it…. What shall I give my poor little Gary to eat? He'll starve. He's thin as a stick insect…. Lend us a fiver Kath.

KATH: Love to Lill, only I'm in Queer Street meself; backs to the wall, har har.

LILL: Nao. Go on Kath, you've always got money from somewhere, meters or other people's pockets.

KATH: Cheeky cow. I ain't got the price of a penny bloater. Get the kettle on Lill…. Matter of fact love, I've just seen something in me catalogue that you'd've loved.

LILL: What's that Kath?

KATH: Stylish pair of winter boots in Alaskan bison hide. Look … lovely … only eighteen quid. They'd've covered up your veins Lill, get you loads of fellers…. What a shame you lost your book.

LILL: Aow. Beautiful. A girl could commit murder for a pair like that.

KATH: A girl?

LILL: Only I could never wear them. Me legs swell.

KATH: Nao. They stretch. Says here 'fit any leg'.

LILL: I could have another look for me book.

KATH: Let's see…. Hey, what's behind the cushion? Here it is. Bit chewed up though.

LILL: That bleedin' dog must've buried it there.

KATH: No it's all right, you can still see it's your name on it. Look, Lilian April Mansell…April?

LILL: My middle name. My Mum thought it was beautiful.

KATH: You ain't nothing like bleedin' April. She should've called you Nofuckingvember…. Come on Lill. Get down that Post Office. Then we'll have a bit of a celebration. Like a nice pair of boots, crying out for the caress of your toes…. Fiver down and then I'll see you once a week for six months.

LILL: Thanks Kath. You are good to me. Tell you what, I'll buy you a drink down the Prince o' Wales.

KATH: All right Lill. Mine's a rum and black. Don't mind how rum they are, don't care if they're black, har har.

Much of it was facile and contrived, but I had never laughed so much as when we were writing. We got away with it because at that time the improvident had not yet become objects of political hatred. They were also figures from our own past; and we thought we had a right to treat them without mercy, because we knew them; although we sensed that those for whom we were writing did not. We didn't permit this to inhibit us.

It now looks different. We were present at the consolidation of new forms of class: we had become part of a liberal upper middle class, which we mistook for radicalism; while the unreconstructed working class would become increasingly conservative, reluctant to change, angry and bewildered at the ending of a homogeneous culture and the fragmentation of the working class through migration into Britain from the Caribbean and South Asia, and the decay of the historic mission sometimes attributed by certain political theorists to the workers. We actually contributed to the separation of the upwardly mobile from those we thought we had 'left behind'; a shift that would be more clearly defined only with the coming of Thatcherism. This would erase the culture of the women we wrote about, whom we endowed with the archaic sensibility of a generation we knew only too well. If we thought those we were writing about did not understand the changes they were passing through – and which were passing through them – their ignorance was slight compared with ours. Half a century on, many have become wiser; and have learned to recognise both their false friends and their true enemies.

Like the communities which we were leaving, we recognised, neither our role in the losses involved in our departure, nor the gains which migrants brought in the vital occupations they filled and in the vibrancy their culture breathed into a decaying provincialism.

ऋ ॐ

For a time life in the gin palace was pleasant enough; although eventually Alastair became resentful of the time Michael and I were spending together, providing us with enjoyments from which he was excluded. It was not that he had other plans for Michael; but I became more of an irritant. The time dedicated to our 'writing' was chaotic and unstructured, and involved lots of papers lying around. This drove Alastair into a disproportionate fury. Even a book left out on a table overnight would be meticulously shelved by the morning, if, indeed, it had not been carried out to the communal dustbin with the potato parings and the remains of the pork chops from the previous day's dinner.

But an even greater source of discord came from the political differences between us. Alastair's benefactor was South African and had been a firm defender of the apartheid regime. One evening we went to a concert of Miriam Makeba at the Albert Hall. She sang about black Africans owning a miserable 15 per cent of the land in which they were the vast majority. Alastair became angry and walked out of the performance. What right had she, he wanted to know afterwards, to come to Britain and perform her political bias in public? After that, we became more careful not to talk of anything which would throw Alastair into a rage. This meant that our domestic conversation became more trivial and more stilted, unless loosened with the help of the increasingly prevalent culture of domestic dependency on alcohol. As this happened, the un-ironed socks and the misplaced teaspoon assumed an ever greater importance. Tension rose. Where I was supposed to have brought a healing balm to the asperities of the relationship between Michael and Alastair, Michael was finding impossible demands made upon his slight diplomatic skills to prevent Alastair's pent-up resentment from expressing itself with the severity all the years of institutional repression had fostered in him. Michael had, from the beginning, set up a kind of social and intellectual infidelity to his partner, which could not long endure.

The time of the week I liked least was Saturday night, for this was when the house was pervaded by the compulsions of obligatory fun. This meant going out separately to find casual sex, proficiency in which always eluded me. The house was full of the oppressive scent of after-shave and deodorant; talcum powder was trodden into the bathroom carpet; the tang of Imperial Leather soap and Herbal Essences shampoo lingered. I would have preferred to stay in and work; and sometimes I would watch Michael to see whether he was prepared to forgo the ritual of standing in the Coleherne or the Boltons in Earl's Court, waiting to make eye contact with the night's prospective partner. More often than not, he would be leafing through his diary, reminding himself of who he knew, to save the hassle of starting afresh. This image remained with me: he did not know, or could not remember, who he liked and with whom he fancied spending the night; so slender was his attachment to people that he needed a name and phone number before he could even visualise who they were.

When each had followed his individual trajectory, I sometimes stayed at home, listening to the 19th-century French clock with its black marble pillars and gold face, ticking heavily on the marble mantelpiece. Occasionally, since I was wise enough to know that this was the meaning of liberation, I would also make my way to one of the pubs, with their tessellated floors, great red wooden counters and engraved glass doors, to try my luck with those more knowing and more experienced than I was. Perversely, if someone asked me the time, I would point up to the clock to demonstrate that this was no way to initiate a conversation. I still felt the weight of my mother's implication that I was so repelling and so monstrous that no one but she would ever tolerate, let alone love, me. I would always place myself at a distance, as though saying to people that they must surely have made a mistake and could certainly do better if they tried; a lesson swiftly understood.

Occasionally, undeterred, someone would persist. We would go by bus to his bedsit in Leytonstone or, if I was lucky, Chiswick; and we would take an occasional glance sideways for an appraisal of our success. Once we arrived, treading heavily up the thin-carpeted stairs, after a powdered coffee and a Marie biscuit, I would politely ask where his family came from. An Italian man one night said, 'Rome.' I replied, 'Oh I adore Rome, I love those little Romanesque churches that are buried like cellars in out of the way places. There's one with a little gem of a Giotto that no one knows about.' He looked at me with bewildered anger and said, 'If I wanted a fucking lecture I'd go to night school.' And then followed a sad journey on the last bus, as the windows streamed with condensation and the cold numbed my feet and chilled my body. I thought I had to impress by my erudition or wit, since I possessed few other charms; I did not realise, as Michael did, that tense silences and a suggestion of pent-up sexual passion were the means to arouse people. I would hear the front door bang at five in the morning and wonder at his capacity to attract people so easily; longing, but scarcely daring, to ask his secret, because he might then accuse me of invading what he called his 'private life', on the edge of which his reticence was as sharp and clear as barbed wire and No Trespassing signs.

Alastair and he had what they called an 'open relationship'; an arrangement which, it was understood by gay men, permitted them to seek sexual experience wherever they chose, but which was not supposed to put at risk emotional intimacy; for which neither Michael nor Alastair seemed to have much of a gift; and so they frequently brought home their partner of the night. Sunday mornings were spent with strangers over cornflakes and coffee, making careful conversation to people who might have been ballet dancers or bricklayers: the only way to be sure which was which was to assume the butch men with stubby fingers were the dancers and the ephebes with a cascade of blond hair were in the building trade.

At one point Alastair met someone he said he had fallen instantly in love with; a marketing manager who, within days, had moved into the house, making of the spare triangular relationship an instant rectangle. This was deeply disturbing to

Michael because his relationship with Alastair was based on the premise that love did not exist, and was therefore seen as an infringement of the eccentric contract they had made. There followed a period of great turbulence, a rather inelegant quadrille. Since the house belonged to Alastair, we were bound, by the laws of hospitality, to be polite to the young man who was under his protection as 'guest'.

It didn't last long, since Gerard, the interloper, was such a fervent adherent of open relationships that the doors of his heart were apparently flung wide to all comers, and one evening he brought home two supplementary partners, which offended Alastair's sense of propriety, and he asked him to leave.

ജ ര

Perhaps Alastair should have known better. It was, after all, the time of gay liberation. The meetings at the London School of Economics attracted gay men in great numbers, and passionate speeches and debates were to be heard, of great crusading zeal. Gay men would show a buttoned-up straight society the true pathway to sexual emancipation; and the rights of even the most transgressive forms of sexual activity were vigorously championed. The unthinking dogma, 'if it moves, fuck it', was seriously advocated by people who, when they were not caught up in the intoxicating compulsions of liberation, were university lecturers, bank personnel, scientists, engineers and lawyers.

Our relative indifference to this social movement was paradoxical but of a piece with the absence of involvement in wider politics. While we retained a frozen allegiance to the left – and still expected the Labour Party to announce its passionate commitment to a radically different world from that in which we lived – we were also very busy cultivating our relationship with the one in which we were so comfortable, hoping to gain a recognition which it continued to withhold. We eagerly sought acknowledgement of the talents we had been led to believe (by whom or by what?) it had detected in us; and the modest degree of success we enjoyed only served as a taunt and a stimulus to further effort.

Gay Liberation did not seriously disturb this relationship with the existing order, from the promises of which we expected so much. These reflections suggest that a society which offers people a great deal in the way of hope – however vain this might prove to be – readily undermines people's desire for radical change. In any case, the dynamic of the attachment between us absorbed so much energy, so much of the emotion we thought we had conquered, that our friendship stood in the way of a deep commitment to the gay movement which we might otherwise have felt.

In spite of this I joined a group affiliated to Gay Lib called Icebreakers. This was a telephone service for troubled, hesitant or uncertain gay men. Lesbians had little part in this at the time. Gay men assumed, perhaps, that the women's movement furnished adequate scope for all women, and gay men remained for the time apart.

At Icebreakers we would listen sympathetically to whatever callers had to say, counsel them in the ways of sexual freedom, and invite them to what were called 'tea-parties' on Sunday afternoons at the home of the members of the collective.

This did indeed perform a valuable service. We posted stickers with the number of the helpline all over London, and later in the Midlands and the North, in Scotland and Wales. The calls were taken in a scruffy office in Brixton on Atlantic Road, a room above a derelict shop. This seemed an appropriate location for an unexpectedly extensive population of people who were frightened, had denied their sexual orientation for years, been unaware of it until the present discussions took place, or who despised or hated themselves for the aberration they thought they were. Many lived in villages and small towns where they had never knowingly spoken to another gay person. Some led lives of impeccable respectability and feared blackmail, exposure and being known as 'perverts'. One man was the head of a Social Services department of a London borough. I asked him if he had told his wife. He said it would kill her. This was a common response – wives or mothers would not survive the disclosure of these terrible secrets. I stopped saying things like, 'There has been no recorded death of anyone because of someone else's sexual predilections,' since statements about the fatal consequences of knowledge for the women who loved them were metaphors for their own absence of confidence or security.

The Sunday afternoon tea-parties were also sadly instructive: the arm scarred with self-inflicted cigarette-burns or deep cuts from a carving knife; the self-neglect; the tears of the schoolteacher terrified of being outed; the father blackmailed by a former lover until he had had to abandon his family and sell his house; the attempted suicide; the loneliness and fear, the unspoken love and broken spirit; the unmet need and the friendlessness of so many people, some of whom travelled from Wolverhampton or Leeds for the sake of a couple of hours of being acknowledged by those who would neither judge nor blame.

The ethos of Icebreakers was not to behave like social workers. This laudable ambition was all very well; but many of those involved regarded it as their duty to initiate many of the men into gay relationships (with themselves), particularly if they were young and attractive, as many indeed were. Assignations were made, friendships sometimes developed, but at the same time, some encounters had no sequel, and the attendees at the tea-parties went back to their Lincolnshire village or their Lancashire town feeling deceived or abused by those they had expected to help them. And although I recognised that this was a betrayal, I did not have the confidence to say so, since any departure from the doctrines of liberation would have invited accusations of being closeted and self-oppressed.

Michael had the greatest contempt for such activities, finding a perfectly satisfactory pool of active and available gay men for his own purposes. He was moralistic: I was only in Icebreakers because in the misery of others I could drown my own sense of failure.

There was, no doubt, some truth in this. But I had not yet understood that Michael also found some kind of satisfaction in my inadequacies. I told him everything about my adventures in the alternative country of Gaytonia, which is what we might have called the altered circumstances in which we lived. I adopted the familiar tone in which we had belittled all our social encounters; although I should perhaps have reflected that for Michael this was the one area of life in which mockery was prohibited. While he may have scorned the liberationist rhetoric, that did not mean he did not take the arena of sexuality (and it was for him, a kind of arena, in which 'performance', at several levels, was paramount) very seriously indeed.

&ᄋ �

Perhaps this is why I regarded Michael as a kind of profane confessor at this time, a contorted residuum, perhaps of his Catholic upbringing. In the exciting days of partial decriminalisation it was inevitable that gurus should be sought who would point out the far from narrow path to new forms of virtue, and he was generous with his advice.

The legislation of 1967, which decriminalised sexual relationships between males over the age of twenty-one in private, certainly meant emancipation for gay men of that age and over, as was evident in all the gay clubs and bars that celebrated their opening, not only in major cities, but also in smaller towns and urban areas where such amenities had previously been unimaginable. The Gay Liberation movement gave rise to much passionate discussion on the nature of sexuality, the limits of tolerance, the legacy of past repression, the lower age at which young people were becoming sexually active and the need for further reform.

The euphoria this created, however, did not always reach those who most needed it, especially older people who had grown up in an atmosphere of shame and self-denial. Michael and I were affected differently. Michael had never permitted legal prohibition to inhibit him, although he never dispelled a deep sense of guilt, partly an inheritance of his Catholic childhood and partly a need to exhibit his working-class authenticity, which, for him, required rigorous suppression of unorthodox proletarian habits. I, on the other hand, had taken very seriously what were regarded as the criminal tendencies which our legislature had detected in gay men, and this had been reinforced by the diffuse but effective condemnation of sex with which my mother – traumatised by her own experience – had saturated the childhood of me and my brother.

The psychological consequences of what had been a proscribed identity were not swept away by the lifting of legal restraints; although it did permit Michael to intensify and to proselytise his already exuberant belief in sex as salvation. I remained far more cautious; and I looked to Michael as my guide in these newly opened pathways to emancipation.

I had a brief relationship with Christophe, a young man from Mauritius. He was very likeable, articulate and intelligent. We spoke French together. He was Catholic and had been subjected to a religious severity which only colonial authorities knew how to inflict with the degree of violence required to crush all traces of anterior faiths or cultures. A consequence of this was that after sex he always wept; not in a noisy or conspicuous way, but rather in sad memory of the belief he could neither entirely live up to nor abandon completely. It did not seem strange or eccentric; but even I must have known that confiding this secret to Michael was an act of spectacular unwisdom. I think our friendship depended upon my deference to him in sexual matters, since without it, the relationship would have collapsed. I therefore colluded in my own – alas, all too familiar – sense of inferiority, and invited Michael onto the lean pastures of the affections, telling myself (actually I didn't tell myself anything, I just acted) that these were trivial matters, set against the destiny that we still believed awaited us.

Accordingly, Michael waited for a moment when there were several friends gathered around the dinner table. If this sounds rather grand, it certainly was. Alastair did not do things by half measure. The crystal goblets, the silver service, the immaculate tantalus with its decanters locked against absent inferiors, the candelabras were worthy of a medieval banquet. Alastair, although severely practical, even prosaic, let his imagination run wild within the safe confines of approved special occasions.

Michael duly delivered his revelation about Christophe during the fish-course (yes, we actually had seven separate courses, including, to finish mushrooms on toast). I had never before attended such a sumptuous feast. Christophe replaced his knife and fork, and, without a word, fetched his coat, and left. I never saw him again. Michael pretended to be astonished at such a reaction; and the rest of the banquet was conducted in an even more stilted silence than usually attended such ceremonial refections.

Only then, I think, did I realise that there was something – irregular – about my relationship with Michael. But I didn't know what to do about it. It was, after all, such fun, those long days – preferably when it was raining – where we created our gallery of working-class women and teenagers, and set them off on adventures in Deptford, Lewisham or the Bricklayers Arms. If we created a deeply satisfying fantasy world, life still nagged at the fraying fabric of our inventions. Something would surely happen – fame, love or some other form of good fortune in our rather privileged version of the lottery of life. Significantly, a sudden access of immense riches was not one of them. It wasn't that I 'allowed myself' to prolong our conspiracy – I actively promoted it, and accepted the disadvantages willingly enough for the sake of the considerable consolations on which we had both, in our way, become dependent.

Michael's was a very protean personality. As a matter of fact, he was known by several names, according to the class and sensibility of his acquaintances. To some he was known as Mike; sunny, ordinary, take me as you find me. Others called him Spike, a name he had assumed in his early excursions into provincial low life: this was used to pretend he was a bit of rough. I would answer the phone, and a voice of great refinement would ask, apprehensively, 'Is Spike there?' Sometimes I would say, 'No, he's working on the oil-rigs,' or 'He's down the pub.' Slightly relieved, the voice would say 'Could you tell him Dominic called? No need to ring back. I'll try later.' Sometimes he was Mikey; loveable, cuddly, everybody's friend. There was Mick, frivolous, working-class, witty, and there was Mr O'Neill; an official personage, schoolteacher and pillar of the community. It all suggested a crowd of people. I never met most of them.

One of these alien characters was a dedicated disrupter of marriages. This may have had its origin in his father's disturbance of the relationship with his mother in his early years. It is difficult to be sure; but it was a pattern repeated many times. He had many 'girl-friends', mostly married women, teachers or social workers. He would give them to understand that he knew all about their unhappiness ('Oh Michael, how could you ever guess, I've never told anyone'); and that, given their desperately conventional lives in Hadley Wood or Chislehurst, they must be doing great violence to their instincts by their mindless persistence in monogamy, when a whole world of excitements beckoned from beyond the French windows and lawns of their comfortable domesticity. He made it clear to them that he, untutored child of the proletariat (despite his Cambridge education), might be their rescuer. 'Oh Michael,' they said, 'How can you know what it's like, how painful it has been, how sad a life without love?' They saw in him wonderful depths of experience and insight, and over a period of two or three years might actually agree to forsake the family hearth and set up in a flat in Lewisham, or somewhere equally inner-city, and risk everything on a new beginning with this seductive but strangely elusive charmer.

This happened two or three times in his adult life. It was not a conscious project, but lay in a profound need to revise constantly his childhood sense of what he felt was his mother's desertion. It was, like so many of our vain attempts to make good the irreversible, a sad and sterile effort, since clearly, none of the women had the slightest understanding of the mythic past, in the re-enactment of which they were to have a major role. All he had to do was to hint suggestively that there was much more he could say, but would forbear to do so in order not to hurt their feelings. They were bowled over. Once the work had been done, he would distance himself or, if it were becoming too burdensome, tell them they had only themselves to blame and goodbye.

Michael was always cavalier with appointments, especially with those – both men and women – who would, he was certain, do anything for him. He would make an assignation at a restaurant in Soho for seven o'clock, and arrive at eight fifteen, knowing she would still be there. He would then enact the scene for us later that night.

Lydia*, fretful, would say, 'Oh Michael. I was just going. Where on earth have you been? I've drunk a whole carafe of

---

* Lydia is a composite character, amalgam of several people.

wine. I booked the table for seven. I had to give Giuseppe two pounds not to sit anyone else at the table.'

'I forgot. I fell asleep in the bath.'

'Oh Michael, no. How ghastly. I did that once after I had taken some Nembutal. I just managed to get the plug out with my toe.'

'No, I hadn't taken anything. I just felt relaxed.... You don't seem very pleased to see me.'

'I don't think I am now. Two hours ago I needed you desperately, but now I'm not so sure.'

'Your face is all puffed up.'

'Yes I know. I can't help it. I've been crying.'

'Oh yes.' After a pause, while Michael examined the menu, Lydia said 'Don't you want to know why?'

'Oh look, clams in white sauce. I love them.... Why?'

'I had a ghastly day at work. I was attacked by a girl. Schizophrenia.'

'I expect you drove her to it.'

'She had a knife Michael.'

'Did she use it? You look pretty unscarred.'

'And then I get home to discover that the police have been to see Victor. Drugs. He's fifteen.'

'Oo, could he get me some?'

'You don't understand. He's going to be expelled, there's going to be ghastly scandal.... A mother's guilt, you'd never understand, how could you?'

'Is that the end of the catalogue of woe? Can we have some food?'

'I think I'm going to divorce Edwin.'

'What for?'

'He's crazy.... He's been in analysis for seven years ... I don't think I can take much more of it.... I can't see any point in living like this. One day I shall do something silly.'

'You do something silly every day.'

Lydia burst into noisy tears. 'I can't bear it. I can't bear it. How can you be so cruel and horrible?'

'If you don't shut up, I'm walking out, and you can carry on with your monologue. You've got your audience. I shouldn't think they need to go to the theatre now.'

Lydia sniffed.

'Pass the menu Michael.'

ༀ ༀ

The life Michael and I shared independently of Alastair created an enclave in the purposeful and orderly routine of the household, an oasis of shiftless and untidy excitement. We found immense enjoyment writing plays, mainly for radio. It was now the early seventies. Michael's role as working-class hero ought to have been fading. But an urchin allure persisted, and it is always difficult for us to set aside the familiar persona we have come to know, if not necessarily love. Michael could scarcely any longer distinguish between the projected self and the protected self; and, if anything, it was the latter which was losing definition. He was helped in this by the prodigious capacity for masochism among women, like Lydia, of the liberal middle class. Even as social antagonisms receded in society in general, Michael clung to them with greater intensity, for it was here that our identity had been forged (in both senses of the word). Later he became more goblin than elfin; but, like some ancient *jeune premier*, he could not give up the role in which he had made his name, and appeared before his fans, a quavering Romeo in his infirmity.

In any case, the true voice of a significant section of the working class was that of Alastair, who freely expressed his disdain for those who would later come to be stigmatised as a 'metropolitan elite'. This was a concept which Michael would have found outrageous at that time; though, in later years of declining health, when his principal diversion was extravagant cruises to places of which he had once studied the anthropology, he would, no doubt, have recognised himself as belonging to that category, despite his reluctance to admit it.

Whenever I think of the past, I cannot imagine now how I remained for so long a far-from-innocent bystander at the relationship between Michael and Alastair. Even at the time I was mystified by the durability of their relationship – they lived together for about six years. Clearly political compatibility played no part in it. My role was to divert and provide stimulus for Michael which would otherwise have been lacking. We actually formed a caricature of an already-archaic family group. Michael was not displeased to observe the antagonism between me and Alastair, since he was the cause of our mutual antipathy. I naturally saw myself as peacemaker; despite the fact that both Alastair and Michael thrived on turbulence, and my efforts were annulled by the stormy scenes they played out together. These reminded me of the more repressed domestic abuse of my childhood. There was one particular Bank Holiday in South London when Alastair had decided to decorate the house himself. It was cold. Michael asked if we could have some heating on. 'It's April 10th,' said Alastair, in an emphatic tone that suggested the seasonal timetables of a railway company took priority over a recognition of existing weather conditions. He said unsympathetically, 'A bit of physical effort and you'll both get warm.' He said we were going to the paint the bedrooms and then go down to the garden centre to see about some exotic plant that sounded like *Maxiflora grandiphylla* for the conservatory. He invited us to look at the colour charts from Homeglow Mural Embellishments. 'I've marked out the ones I like. I want you to choose now.' Thinking I was being conciliatory, I said, 'Oh I don't mind. I like anything.' This turned Alastair's irritation into anger, and Michael made things worse by saying, 'Black and mauve and red and orange…. Look at the fucking names Jerry, Circassian Green, Adobe Ember, Tyrrhenian Blue, Afghan Red….' Alastair said, 'You can start washing down. We'll have my colours. Tyrrhenian Blue and Alhambra Gold.' 'Christ,' said Michael, 'It'll look like the Vatican.'

Alastair exploded. 'You don't care if you live in a piggery, do you? You've been on holiday for a week, and all you've done is tread baked beans into the carpet and miss the lavatory pan every time you go. It's disgusting.' He threw his coffee cup at the wall. It smashed and a liquid stain made a Rorschach blot where the first coat of Tyrrhenian Blue would be applied. I rushed to pick up the broken china saying, in what I imagined was a soothing tone, 'There's no need to get upset over paint.' Michael turned to me and said, 'You shut your fucking mouth. It has nothing to do with paint.' Clearly I was trespassing on a feud in which I had no part. I said I would get to work on preparing the surfaces, and Alastair said he wanted neither of us to have anything to do with it. Michael replied, 'Just because you were brought up in the workhouse doesn't mean we have to live in one.' Alastair thumped Michael, and when I tried to intercede, Michael thumped me and told me to get a life of my own. Then they went upstairs to have sex.

$$\text{\reflectbox{\&}} \quad \text{\&}$$

There were many such symbolic battles; and I learned, at length, to keep out of them, since they represented conflicts which required, not the emollience of an outsider, but resolution from within. But once I had withdrawn from what Michael called my United Nations role, Alastair turned his attentions more completely to making my life even more unbearable than the dark blue walls, sparkling crystal and his prohibition on the display of any reading whatsoever had managed to do. Notes were left pointing out the absence of diligence in my housekeeping skills. Alastair upbraided me for failing to carry out tasks he had never charged me with. He continued to place items of cutlery I had rigorously returned to their appointed place on the surface of the cabinet.

I did not expect Michael to support me and he didn't. He stayed later and later at school, coming home from 'parents' evenings', which went on till nine o'clock three or four times a week. My tête-à-tête meals with Alastair were stilted and formal, where the ticking of the clock and the scraping of cutlery on plates were the dominant sounds. It became obvious, even to me, that it was time to go. But I had never lived on my own. I was only here, as it were, under Michael's threadbare protection. Where would I go? In spite of being a social worker, I was utterly resourceless and devoid of the social skills in which I was supposed to be instructing the truly derelict.

Defeated for at least the third time, I went back to Northampton, the provincial town we had scorned; and I begged it to receive me tenderly, the home-place where wounded feelings are assuaged, failures overlooked, and bruised encounters with the capital city seen for what they are – a rebuff to the homely common sense of real people. I didn't believe any of this, of course, but I was bound to accept the evaluation of the neighbours in Palmerston Road, who looked at me, I thought – or imagined – with malevolent compassion and a myopic shrewdness which assumed I had finally learned my place in the world.

So it was I resigned myself to the desultory role of blacksmith in a one-horse town. It was not that there was nothing to do. An 'expressway' was going to demolish a thousand houses, the 'little palaces', for which generations of shoemakers had led sparing, frugal lives to call their own, sitting over spent coals in mufflers, with a dewdrop on the end of their bony nose, going to bed with the sun so as not to 'burn daylight', scraping a thin layer of margarine on the bread and using the tea-leaves three times before throwing them onto the patch of blighted earth they called their garden. Years of self-denial had at last earned them an austere interior which, whatever its deficiencies, had freed them from the bondage of landlords; and now their modest social mobility was going to be bulldozed for the sake of the greater urgencies of spatial mobility. They were having none of it.

A group was formed – Labour councillors, reporters from the local paper, some old Northampton radicals – which vowed to halt the project. Street committees were assembled, collections made, meetings held. Hundreds of people attended the Co-Op Hall, where I had made my debut as Othello twenty years earlier, and where it was possible, for the first time in a popular assembly to rail against the 'tyranny of progress' in the name of humanity – a valuable political lesson that has, perhaps, remained largely unlearned by progressives, even today, in the presence of populism, nativism and renascent fascism.

This also provided me with a new understanding of the relationship between the capital and the provinces. As one of a generation of people who, from all over Britain (as indeed, Europe and the USA), had forsaken their home town at the earliest opportunity, I could see – precisely in these deserters – an absent dynamic leadership which might have radically altered the nature and thrust of local government, had their profession, career or ambition not called them away to more compelling metropolitan or international occupations. This was not, of course, a personal, but rather, a systemic, characteristic. But it does help account for the years of neglect and indifference which made the people of many towns and cities feel they had been abandoned; an abandonment the more poignant for having been inflicted upon them by their own children, for whom the home town remained a place they revisited to spend Christmas with their parents, to allow them to spoil their grandchildren for a few days, and finally, were called back to, following the cancer diagnosis, the fall in the garden, the need for a nursing home. Vastly forgiving, the ageing relatives gave them a permanent alibi: 'You have your own lives to lead,' 'I've had my time and now it's your turn.' The bitterness they felt shifted, so that it was no longer concentrated on the defecting individuals, but became entangled with social, political and economic changes they had never willed, and for which they were later to seek redress; not always appropriately, since it had not been Labour politicians who had initiated the disruptions and discontinuities; although these might, perhaps, have articulated them more clearly, had they had the insight to do so.

ஐ ௸

This time, going home and taking part in an overtly political project, was a richly instructive experience. I was elected as councillor for one of the wards most affected by the scheme; and although the 'expressway' became only a shrunken version of the original plan, this was caused more by budgetary constraints than by the effectiveness of our campaign.

When I think now of my brief stint as representative for St Crispin (the patron saint of shoemakers) Ward, I feel an intense sadness, both for the hope that the poor and elderly people of that neighbourhood placed in the Labour Party, and for my failure to make any significant contribution to their position. I remember my 'adoption' meeting (political orphan that I was), where the declining membership of no more than seven or eight people listened to my wholly inappropriate and impassioned plea for their support. The meeting was in a terraced house converted into Labour Party offices, a stuffy and chaotic room with gunmetal filing cabinets, Windsor chairs and a desk stained with the rings of mugs of coffee consumed many years before. It was 1972 and I chose a denunciation of the 'progress' that would sweep away many small houses. I railed against an affluence of which few of my constituents had experienced as anything more than a rumour. I can still see the face of one retired shoe-worker, who looked at me through smeared spectacles which had been mended with a piece of wire, who, bewildered, asked why when they had for years been asking for a greater share of the national pie, were now being asked to demand less of it. I did not recognise how far I had travelled from the sensibility of those I thought I was going to represent. People looked at me as though I had just arrived from some exotic culture, which, in a way, I had.

At the time it didn't feel like this. I was beginning to accept that my return home might this time be definitive, and that I might never again leave. But I wondered where, among the ageing membership of the Labour Party and the remnants of amateur dramatic societies (now that going to London for a night at the theatre was within reach of most who wished for it), would I find solace and sympathy, let alone stimulus and affection. Would I, after all, finish my life as an alderman of this county borough, being feted in the Victorian town hall for my contribution to the erasure of the local sensibility that had formed me, the dereliction of the town centre and the emergence of what, in more senses than one, would become a dormitory town, site of an even sounder sleep than the somnolence of a defunct provincialism? Would I live in sexless exile in a fabricated respectability, sedately walking my dog and acting as judge at the annual flower and vegetable show in the park? I could almost see the earwigs falling out of the dahlia blooms and hear the caterpillars eating to a lacy filigree the outer leaves of the cabbages, as I walked through the scent of trampled grass in the mildewy tents awash with August rain. I felt reclaimed; as though I had reached for something beyond my grasp, and had fallen back into the wet grass clutching a few leaves and twigs while the golden apple still shimmered, out of reach, on the tree.

I did not need to wonder how Michael felt at this time. I knew he would be dying of boredom. Part of my flight home had been in order to punish Michael's failure to defend me against Alastair. I felt my role, as human glue to keep together the fragile relationship, although voluntarily assumed, entitled me to a consideration I ought to have known better than to expect. I felt both virtuous and vengeful, an unattractive mixture, tempered, perhaps, by a sense of guilt that I had abandoned Michael. Our collusive silence facilitated many mutual betrayals which we were constrained to accept without protest, however they may have wounded us.

Michael came to Northampton one weekend and offered his scathing admiration for my political activism. He was gloomy. I asked how business was in the gin palace. We finally admitted to each other that we missed – not friendship (that would have been too much), but play-writing – and that the life we had apparently opted for was stifling. With a sense of immense relief, verging on a joy well-dissimulated, we decided there *was* something we could do about it. Of course, it was an unbalanced decision, and when we agreed that our sacrifices would be virtually equivalent if Michael left Alastair and I abandoned what passed for radical politics in our town, I didn't point out that this might even up the score of treachery between us. I had no particular wish to punish Alastair, but I had no affection for him. My attachment was to Michael; and I scarcely paused to reflect upon the possible grief of Alastair if Michael fled yet another of the scenes he had created but which had become onerous to him. As it turned out, Alastair showed no sign of particular emotion; but had, in any case, been taught never to do so. He simply made it clear that Michael could take nothing but his clothes and personal effects. 'That's all right,' said Michael, who at that time qualified all possessions as demonic, 'I don't mind if I leave stark naked.'

The expressway having been much reduced, the planning blight that had eaten away at many of the little Victorian houses was lifted, and their value rose a little once more. But the whole district had been damaged; with the result that most of the houses were soon occupied by transients, the homeless, families preceded by the word 'problem' as though this were an adjective; safety-pins held ill-matching curtains together, squares of cardboard covered broken panes; the paint flaked and was not renewed; doorsteps crumbled. The life in the streets that had held people together in neighbourly unity ebbed.

There were a few hundred pounds left in the fund; and this was donated to Shelter. I was actually evicted from the council for non-attendance at meetings; and many of the worthy people whose houses we had protected from demolition assumed, with the misanthropic charity of those who had always been cheated, that I had run away to London with a fabulous sum of money, with which I would no doubt live the life of Riley in the West End – this being the only district of London which they knew to be haunted by those most stigmatised and reprehensible people, seekers after pleasure.

ℰ꘎ ꙅ

So Michael and I went to live in a rented – and only nominally furnished – flat in Herne Hill.

This was the most Spartan and exiguously appointed dwelling imaginable. It was on the top floor of what had been luxurious apartments when they were built in the 1930s. There were still vestiges of former elegance – green-tiled bathrooms with unlimited hot water from a central boiler, a slate fireplace, elegant door- and window-fittings; although the metal of the latter had become somewhat corroded, so that the flimsy curtains ballooned into the rooms in the slightest breeze. The furniture was cheap and fragile, the floors covered in red and yellow linoleum. Thin metal chairs around a narrow plastic table which could barely accommodate two cups and a teapot, narrow beds which would have made the most ascetic medieval religious immediately renounce their vows and return to the comfort of their cells; a sofa that sat prim as a strait-laced aunt in the corner, and two yellow chairs that might, in another context, have been called easy.

We loved it. This was an environment to relish – no labour, no duties, no housekeeping; only improvised meals, cups of tea and bottles of wine. We never cleaned the floor, with the result that dust didn't accumulate, but formed whorls of tumbleweed which raced beneath the furniture in the draught. Only when it looked as though the room were littered with grey scalps we scooped it up and disposed of it. We lived on leeks, bacon and baked beans, and rarely picked up anything that dropped on to the floor. One evening we had run out of cash. We searched through the debris scattered throughout the flat, and found we had eighty pence in one- and two-penny coins that had rolled under the dust; just enough for a bottle of Valpolicella to sustain us, as we produced some swiftly forgettable episode for a TV series or a radio play. The future promised to be without constraint or responsibility.

It was great fun. This was Michael at his best – mischievous, spontaneous, charismatic. He had a capacity for enthralling people, an ability to charm and to entertain, for which there was great scope in the early seventies, which looked at first as if it would simply be an extension of the fancy-dress fantasy of the sixties.

And people came. Life was crowded, in a way it had never been before. Lydia was often there, apparently insatiable for more of Michael's abrasive insights, and there were teachers from Michael's school, actors and gay acquaintances who came and went so quickly we scarcely had time to learn their names. We thought this was liberation; and occasionally, a troupe of our friends would snake into nearby Ruskin Park with a picnic basket and enjoy convivial summer evenings until the park-keepers threatened to close the metal gates on us; than which, we assured them, there was nothing we would like better, so please feel free to go home and leave us to enjoy ourselves.

We never quarrelled. We shared a view of the world which neither seriously disputed or questioned; and because our emotions had, as it were, gone underground, as true subversives often do, the injuries we did one another were never acknowledged, and were met with no visible reaction.

It was clear, however, that this version of emancipation was not without certain disadvantages. Michael had, as a matter of course, appropriated what was known as the 'master-bedroom'. He had said, 'You know that I have enormous needs, sexually, and they have to be respected. There's nothing worse than sexual repression. That is what causes aggression, violence and fascism.' In that case, I objected feebly, I ought to be the most ardent Nazi on earth.

So the flat came to reflect this central premise. The narrow bedframe was replaced by a sort of ceremonial platform in the middle, with posts and a canopy, and resembled the site of the lying in state of one of the last dead monarchs in Europe. On the walls were erotic pin-ups by Touko Laaksonen – men wearing boots and leather jackets, sullen promises of pleasure on the full lips of their clean-shaven faces. A tiger-pelt on the wall above the bed suggested a feral carnality, while a plaster replica of Michelangelo's *David* and two *Kraft durch Freude* figurines on the mantelpiece suggested that there were other pathways to fascism than suppressed sexuality. Nocturnal refreshment, in the form of amyl nitrate was always at hand on the bedside table.

Mine was the small room as far away from this central celebratory chamber as it could be. Michael's needs were ubiquitous. They hovered in the air, inescapable, vulture-like, in perpetual quest for appeasement on the savage altar, on which black sheets were spread like cerements.

Sometimes he talked to me about sexual emancipation and urged me to follow his example. He took me on a tour of the places to go to meet people. 'It's a pity you're not a bit younger and not better-looking,' was his judgement. 'Then you might stand a better chance.' This, of course, meant that I was scarcely fit to show myself in the pubs, discos or bars he indicated; and I rarely did, for to have done so might have cramped his multiple styles and the characters they projected.

We both drank a great deal. This had the advantage of allowing Michael to ascribe to the influence of alcohol any misbehaviour or unkindness. Alcohol and his formidable needs provided him with absolution from responsibility for any of his actions. These were felt to be great impersonal forces, against which mere volition retreated, powerless. His own friends treated me with distant curiosity, which made me feel uncomfortable. They looked as though they knew things about me of which I was not myself aware. This was because Michael had told them on no account to mention sex, because I had an aversion to it, and it would certainly upset me. I suffered from an ill-defined neurasthenia, and in any case, he told them, he only reads Proust.

If I brought anyone to the flat – which occurred infrequently – Michael treated them with disdain. 'Who was that?' he would ask, as though contact with anyone I had made an independent relationship with was out of the question. They were horribly reactionary, ghastly or very unattractive. It became clear to me that the only people I could attract were the unworthy and the inferior. In an echo of my relationship with my mother, Michael gave me to understand that it was solely out of his capacious humanitarianism that he could tolerate my friendship; and I was bound to show him the same gratitude with which I had received the sorrowful and disinterested love of my mother. I could not, of course, articulate this to myself at the time.

ဆာ ဟ

Janet visited us at weekends, although she had reached the point where she could travel only by bus, so her journeys would take two or three hours. I was at this time a social worker with the Elfrida Rathbone Society, a charity which worked with the families of children who had what are now called 'learning difficulties', but in that less squeamish era, were known as 'educationally sub-normal'. These were divided into two categories (M) for Mild and (S) for Severe. The area from which the children came included the part of Hackney where Janet was then installed in a council flat. One day I saw her from a distance. She was wheeling the shopping trolley, which had become indispensable to her mobility. She was hurrying to catch a bus. Her movements were jerky and uncertain. Some children, amused by her erratic haste, gave her an ironic cheer; but the bus-driver waited. She was wearing a wig, since it had become difficult for her to tie up her hair. The wig was a tangle of wiry auburn curls, which gave her the air of Hasid from Stamford Hill. I marvelled at her apparent indifference to her fall in social status. This was such a long way from what life had promised; but she continued to cast the light of her luminous optimism upon all those whose lives she touched. Even when the streets of Hackney had become places to fear and to avoid, as people invested in double locks and window-grilles, Janet's ground floor flat stood open to visitors. And indeed, the contribution of neighbours, friends and her brother and sister prolonged her independence long after she ought to have been taken into protective care. Where vulnerability had always been her defence against predators, her defencelessness now made her vulnerable. She was robbed twice. The first time, a neighbour, recognising the boy who had broken into the flat, went to his house and shamed him into returning the stolen money. On the second occasion, other neighbours replaced the missing sum, so that she scarcely even knew there had been a burglary.

If Janet's relationships with men were passionate and unpredictable, many of her most stable friendships were with gay men. During her long, debilitating decline, she could depend upon our loyalty. Sometimes we took her to the theatre, only to discover there was no access for wheelchairs, and we had sometimes to lift her into a seat in the stalls. These clumsy manoeuvres never cost Janet her dignity; and she would pretend she was being borne aloft in a palanquin, or declared that she was of such noble birth that her feet must never touch the ground. And how she immersed herself in the performance! If the tears she shed were not all for the protagonists in the play, she could perhaps allow herself to weep for her own growing weakness under cover of the more immediate doom of Phèdre or Antigone.

Responsiveness to the sufferings of others was not confined to the theatre. She was known to many beggars in Islington. She believed implicitly whatever they told her; and when it was pointed out that the man to whom she had just given her last five pounds because he had narrowly escaped with his life when his house burnt down, had instantly disappeared into the betting-shop, she would say that only showed his need of the money was far greater than hers. She befriended a well-spoken professional man who claimed he had lost everything in a city fraud; and a stop was put to the money she paid him regularly out of her slender social security allowance, only when the neighbours became suspicious of his regular appearance on her doorstep on payday.

People in public places often confided in her. Because she walked slowly, looked everyone in the eye with a smile on her lips, she was obviously a safe repository for their secret sorrows and untold griefs.

The last employment Janet had was that of home teacher for the Inner London Educational Authority. This involved visiting the homes of children too sick or too frail to attend school, and bringing to them as much instruction as they were capable of receiving. Janet was extraordinarily inventive. She brought delight and wonder into grimly impoverished flats in Poplar and Whitechapel; and whisked the children's imagination away to inhabit a world of her creation. I went with her once to a flat in Bethnal Green, where Grace, a little girl of about eight, was suffering from cerebral ataxia; a pale, etiolated child, like a flower that had grown without sunlight. Janet was affectionate and patient with her pupil's tantrums. In Grace she saw her own fate; and long after any pretension to education had been left behind, Janet continued to visit until the little girl died.

Janet's life was frugal; her great resourcefulness of mind and memory her great consolation. She did not complain of her poverty, but reviewed with pleasure all that she could do within her slight means. When she lived in the greengrocery in Victoria Park, she took delight in Punjabi conversation with the mother, who, although she had lived a quarter of a century in London, had never before spoken to a white person. Janet knew that austerity did not have to be joyless; and hers was a different kind of poverty from the bitterness of want which surrounded her in Hackney. She had even less money than most of her neighbours; but she had at her disposal resources which they had not. Her life was often unhappy, but it was never miserable.

Janet wrote a novel; but as she could no longer control her hand, I transcribed the words as she dictated them. It was never quite finished. It was the story of her relationship with Caleb; but her eloquent account of the sexual infatuation of a white middle-class woman with a black man who could never be her intellectual equal was unlikely to find favour: it ran counter to the fashionable orthodoxies of the day. Janet poured her own anguish into the story, her powerlessness over the ravages of multiple sclerosis in her body not always distinguishable from the visceral emotions that seemed to emulate it. The work is self-deprecating, intense and poetic, a molten mixture of memory, mind and emotion as she recalled the people she had known – 'Rosina and Santuzza' – were those their real names or were they the heroines of operas she had seen? Giorgio Albertazzi on the record-player – Dante, Petrarch, Leopardi, Carducci – black coffee and Hungarian salami, the future ahead, breathlessly anticipating their arrival, in order to lavish upon them its unguessed-at riches, its dazzling complexity. Tomorrow was their permanent address. She wrote of looking out of a window at the back of college one snowy St Valentine's Day morning, at 'an enormous heart trodden out in the snow on the college hockey-field beneath, and her name in footprints, the designer of this gargantuan piece of ephemera now vanished completely from her memory.... The marvellous Peruvian archaeologist who had kissed her on King's College Bridge in the fog. Narrow pointed willow-leaves dark green against a paler grey – a Japanese print, a morning-after letter from the tale of Genji....' Her voice speaks through the manuscript, her impassioned feeling for literature, painting and Caleb, 'O embroider roses on my heart,' she cried, as she evoked 'the ivory bone beneath the gold satin skin of her lover, and drowning in his eyes, the fishpools of Hebron.'

Janet managed to conceal the extent of her decline for a long time, simply by calling upon a large number of relatives, friends and neighbours in rotation, so that no individual was disturbed frequently enough to become aware of the seriousness of her condition. She might fall, become immobilised in bed, be unable to turn on the gas or manipulate the wheelchair to reach something on a shelf. She would either make do without whatever she required or telephone someone – maybe five or six kilometres away – in order not to alert the neighbours again. In this way, the full gravity of her disability was dispersed among people who rarely met each other, so that there should be no opportunity for them to get together and urge her to action that would be distasteful to her. The ingenuity she had once applied to learning Arabic or Swahili was now deployed upon strategies for daily survival.

৪৩ ৫৪

As her walking became unsteady, she would ask strangers to help her cross the road. She swayed dangerously at the kerbside, and no one knew what desperate effort it cost to retain her balance. Some people avoided her, fearful that her obvious dependency might make excessive calls upon their sparing sympathy or time. Occasionally, she was thought to be drunk or drugged.

One day, as she stood at the edge of a pavement, a young man took her arm. He told her his name was Rachid. He was Moroccan, and working in a restaurant to pay for his studies. She asked him to take her home, and impulsively, asked him in for coffee. He stayed with her for ten months, taking her out, shopping, occasionally going out with her for a meal. It soon appeared that Rachid was an illegal immigrant, having been smuggled into Britain some months earlier in the back of a chilled truck carrying lettuce and tomatoes from Holland.

Janet told him she was forty-eight. He said her eyes told him she was twenty. He was attentive and loving; and this halted for a season the progression of the sclerosis. He prolonged her fragile independence. She was happy.

Rachid stayed in the flat. He returned most nights, but there were unexplained absences. During the summer his boots were often muddy and his hands sore, as though he had been picking fruit or vegetables. In the weeks before he met her, he had been paying rent to sleep in an outhouse, a cold place where the window-frames were stuffed with rags to keep out the draughts. Janet knew better than to ask he give an account of himself, and accepted his comings and goings as the price of the relationship. He never asked her for money, but brought home small offerings – a red rose, a box of North African sweets, some filigree earrings. Without him, Janet would have been forced earlier into the long-stay hospital, which she always referred to as her 'penultimate resting-place'. Rachid was for those brief months both lover and carer, a blend of the fanciful and the practical. 'I don't deserve it,' she said, 'but then, merit has nothing to do with it. I didn't deserve multiple sclerosis.'

Almost a year later, Rachid returned one day, anxious and preoccupied. His disappearances now lasted longer. Unexpected arrivals made him nervous. When Janet's friends called, he vanished, and she made a joke about her phantom lover. I met him only once. He must have been in his mid-twenties, slim, tall, warm. We spoke French. His friends had been growing cannabis in a run-down house near Chatsworth Road, but the police had raided and ransacked the property.

One day, Janet discovered he had taken a small case. His shaving kit and toothbrush had gone from the bathroom. That night he didn't return; or the next.

She was awakened in the early morning by the sound of breaking glass. Suddenly the flat was swarming with police.

Where is he? ... We have reason to believe.... It has been reported.... You are harbouring....

Janet could not get up without help. She told them she was severely disabled, and wondered what crimes they thought her capable of. They found some of Rachid's clothes. 'Who do these belong to?' She told them they were her brother's.

Outside in the indigo dawn, a crowd of neighbours had gathered. They were not well disposed towards the police. 'Poor thing.' 'What's she done, robbed a bleeding bank in her wheelchair?' 'Breaking into the flat of a disabled woman, that's the only crime.' The police asked if she knew someone of a name she had never heard. She told them truthfully that she didn't know him.

She never saw Rachid again. Two months later, she received a post card with no name or address, postmarked Marseille. It said simply 'Thank you.' At the time one of the periodic waves of hysteria about asylum seekers was at its peak. Janet said, 'I sought asylum and he never turned me away.'

ଠ ଔ

Michael was known as an 'inspirational' teacher. He was actually brilliant, especially with children who were 'difficult', who had had a traumatic past or who presented as fiercely intractable. In later life he lived in East Dulwich, not far from where he had taught; and it was startling – and very moving – to observe the number of young women with a train of disorderly children, or boys who looked like apprentice hit-men, and whose impassive faces melted in tender greeting when they saw him. I was with him one day, when a man who turned out to be a bouncer in a night-club seized Michael in a warm embrace. He said, 'Respect this man. He saved my life. If it wasn't for him I'd've been dead meat.' Another boy he had coached freely outside of school hours went to university and entered the civil service. His mother, a Jamaican woman who had lung cancer was an office cleaner, and in her Michael saw his own mother who had cleaned floors for the sake of his education.

Michael would say, 'All you need to educate children is a persuasive voice and a receptive ear'; and these features were always present in his classes. This meant, of course, that with the expansion of a vast education industry, his abilities came to be regarded with suspicion, if not hostility. Without the elaborate apparatus whereby the may-fly attention of the consumers of tomorrow might be captured, you were nothing. Michael's understanding of how to hold thirty adolescents in thrall for an hour no longer counted in an obsessive-compulsive age, where the shiny orthodoxies and the bright-coloured proprieties of progress are defined solely by the lateness of the date on the calendar. Now, heads appeared in the schools where Michael had been employed, and when he declared that he had always been a good teacher, they shook their sagely youthful heads and told him that such was not his purpose. His calling was to facilitate education. He duly went through the prescribed rituals, but did not alter in any particular his teaching methods. His pupils continued to gain grades thought impossible among the deprived population from which they came. For many years, fashion appeased, his method went unchallenged, and he remains a significant figure in the memory of many now-ageing Afro-Caribbean women and men in Peckham.

If I became a social worker, this was because I had deserted the teaching profession principally because of my inability to exercise sufficient control over a class. I made a virtue out of what then required no artificial assistance in goodness, since social workers were then regarded as a species of shepherd, rounding up the stray sheep of progress, and encouraging them into the fold where the pastures of consumption were unwithered by winter chills.

This had at least two advantages. It meant I could locate myself in the advance guard of social progress, but more importantly, I thought I might be able to accommodate myself to my own unhappiness in the presence of the far greater misery of those worse off than myself – a much recommended remedy for self-pity, but profoundly ineffective.

Michael and I had carried with us an archaic notion of poverty, associated with the stories we had taken from our parents – fear of the bailiffs and the Means Test men, the pawned wedding ring and winter coat, the pram full of coal collected from the railway sidings, perforated charity boots and searching the deserted market stalls for the discarded outer leaves of cabbages and mildewed oranges, flitting to avoid unpaid rent and the elderly relative taken out of the workhouse for the day at Christmas; the telegram that told of an only son killed in action in an unpronounceable battle, the young father killed by a dray and the mother who took her own life and that of her two small children.

I expected to be visiting the poorest, and indeed I was. But poverty, that social mutant and master of disguise, was no longer recognisable in the bony shape of penury with which we were familiar. Although our parents had shielded us from it, they were anxious that we should know precisely what we had escaped. They were like refugees desperate to keep alive the oppression from which they had fled, although it bore no relationship to the experience of the children in the sunny land of freedom. We were saturated with a sense of their Edwardian poverty which, for us, became poverty itself.

There had been something heroic the way they had faced destitution; a stoical nobility, a determination to defy and to overcome; an abrasive resistance, and with it, a reservoir of pooled resources on which a community could call. Since then the culture of affluence had passed over the land, and coated the world in its sugary breath; so resistance to that kind of poverty had dissolved, the contrivance and ingenuity with which it had been fought rendered both ineffective and irrelevant. Poverty itself had been transformed – not benignly so; but poverty had ceased to be exclusion and had become simply another – negative – aspect of affluence. It is now a relationship between people and the things they cannot have, rather than a relationship between rich and poor. This is, perhaps, why distaste for the rich has been transformed in popular culture into admiration for their conspicuous wealth.

When I visited homes in East London, I sat on plastic three-piece suites, while a dog clawed at the fabric, children tore open packets of crisps and toddlers sucked at sauce-bottles. Their mother spoke freely before them of her distress and hatred of the bastard who had walked out on her. There was usually a litany of infidelity, desertion, loss, ingratitude, cruelty, the longing to be somewhere else, someone else, a yearning for escape, oblivion, happiness, and above all, sleep, in the noisy watchfulness of an insomniac culture, in which children, alert and hyperactive, no longer enjoyed quiet slumber, but were wide awake, looking for the next thing on which to set their tiny manipulated hearts. It was as though the minute the shining social fabric was touched, it fell apart, not like the material of some ancient tapestry in a closed room, which crumbled to dust when exposed to the air, but because it was about as substantial as cobwebs on an autumn morning.

There were no longer any secrets. People spoke without reticence of what might earlier have been seen as reasons for shame and silence. A new incontinence was in the air. People exhibited their blemishes, their scars, the undescended testicle, the lump in the breast, the blood in the urine. They told of the fear of cancer, the failed abortion, phantom pregnancies and real children. Desolation in the midst of a society overwhelmed by its own anthems and hymns to plenty was an eerie experience; disorienting and rapidly leaving behind the socialist iconography with which we had grown up: a grainy imagery of joyful gymnastics in municipal recreation grounds, community singing and collective celebration of victory in war faded, as people retreated into private spaces, both those rented from the council and the even more inaccessible chambers within.

And everywhere, all public spaces, streets, gardens, houses, parks were inexplicably strewn with waste: bottles for milk, sauce, salad cream, jam; tins of beans, fish, soup, luncheon meat; hardened or mildewed slices of bread fanned out of wrappers; silver-foil trays from the take-away, chicken-bones and red monosodium glutamate; egg-boxes, plastic containers, dispensers of foams, creams, oil, polish, aerosol cans and flacons, casks, cylinders of skin freshener, bath crystals, cosmetics, lotions to make eyes lustrous, to feed hair, cleanse pores, hide blemishes and cover scars; vessels that had contained all the distillations of nature – pure vegetable protein, essential oils of veronica, fennel and jojoba, extracts of chamomile and valerian; sachets of shampoo in which were concentrated all the fruits of the earth, cartons of polish, bottles of bleach, washing up liquid, packets of sweets, cigarettes, newspapers, love magazines, pornography, discarded food and garments – nappies, tights, underwear, torn jeans and soiled dresses, overalls, odd shoes; broken furniture – leg of a coffee table, mattresses blossoming with piss-stains, gnawed bones, pictures, photographs, transistors, long ribbons of spoilt cassettes. In the streets stood skeletons of abandoned cars, stripped of everything that could be used or sold; the roads glittered with glass – fragments of beer bottles, shattered window screens. The waste was strewn on the streets, neglected, a festering reproach to a society eager to discover what lay on the other side of its demolition of the earth.

The debris littering the public areas was reflected inside the houses – broken plastic, dismembered dolls, cars, wheels, guns, trucks, tanks, bicycle frames; comics, rubber swords, dressing-up outfits, as though the fragile identities of infancy already yearned to transcend themselves; board games, playing cards, sweet wrappings, silver paper.

There was another dimension in the used-up materials; a sense of relationships worn out, discarded loves and affections left behind; attachments which, like many of the material things, had already met a more or less violent end; children in care, or gone to live with grandparents or aunts; teenage boys whose association culminated in some spectacular wounding of another; girls 'groomed' by men in their twenties, passed from one adult to another and rewarded with trinkets and clothes; families and kinship fractured like bones; relationships strained by helpless dependencies and love that somehow no longer healed but rather jarred and estranged; new entanglements, fascinations and compulsions that proved no more durable than the perishing objects that furnished both the physical and mental interiors.

All this had nothing to do with the poverty we thought we knew so well – children cowering under old coats instead of blankets to avoid the cold, standing in line at the bakery late at night for stale pastries, or for a penny bloater or a few coals for the empty grate, curtains drawn against the cold at three in the afternoon and children sent to bed so they would think it was night and go to sleep with the help of some tincture of laudanum.

Yet poverty this most surely was. I wondered where we had been – even we, who had prided ourselves on our vigilance – that such mutations could have occurred, unnoticed, as it were, under our very eyes, indeed under the very scrutiny which we had called social observation.

Society, it seemed, had retreated from being the principal determinant in people's lives in favour of the market. And it was the relationship to the market which in turn inflected their

sentiments, feelings, rivalries towards each other. The economics of waste, it seemed, did not spare the people in whose
hands everything fell apart. Although nominally a 'social'
worker, I ought to have been called market trader, dealing,
as I was in the psychic economics of broken human closeness – I gave everything, they cried, and what have I got out
of it? What's in it for me? What have I got to show for it?
Where is the pay-off? Where are the dividends? What miserable returns I got for love, devotion, friendship, duty. I have
been exploited, trampled on, taken for granted. Nothing is
for nothing. You're on your own. Out for number one. Dog
eat dog. The law of the jungle. It was as though the economy
and its growth had burst through the fragile integument of the
human sensibility and contaminated the heart and the spirit
with its irresistible compulsions.

୫୭ ଓଃ

Michael and I continued to write plays; only they were underpinned now by a new kind of instability; an uncertainty that
we any longer understood the social processes we thought
we were documenting. Where our parents had dwelt on the
terrible conditions of their lives, these had been compensated
for by the richness of their collective relationships. Now, it
seemed, as conditions had improved – and at this time, people
living 'on benefit' had not yet been demoted to the grudging
starvelings of a misanthropic system – nothing was wrong
with the world of plenty: it was the spoilt relationships that
blocked our way to it.

I would visit a council flat in an unreconstructed Shoreditch, and mechanically absorb the lament. 'What am I gonna
do? My Sharon's gone to live with a bloke of thirty, she's
only fifteen, he'll be done for abducting a minor, me womb's
shifting about inside me like a balloon on a stick, it's Wayne's

birthday on Tuesday and I ain't seen his dad for two years, the twins lay in bed and do their business, they do it on purpose, if they wasn't coming to turn off the gas tomorrow I'd put me head in the oven.' Feebly, I would say, 'I'll try and get you a holiday through Pearson's fresh air fund.' 'Ow thank you. That'd be lovely. And a bit of spending money for the kids. Not a caravan though, mind, a nice apartment. Thanks.' Our capacity for invention was rapidly falling short of reality.

$$\wp \quad \wr$$

Sometimes Michael stayed away from the flat for several days. He would spend time with an antique dealer or with a traveller on a site on Bromley Common. He had met a Peruvian, a South African, even once an Inuit; he had a list of countries in which he could mark off his triumphs in a growing global gazette. He brought zeal to what he declared an attack on authoritarianism, the life-denying suppression of spontaneous, ubiquitous human sexuality. He insisted that life was about happiness. The real enemy of our natural feelings is a sombre, white male-dominated capitalism, which feeds on aggression, discipline and war.

Michael had shown me where I could meet men on Hampstead Heath. He had, literally, taken me on a tour, demonstrating, like the most accomplished guide, both the diurnal and nocturnal sites of activity, and urging me not to confuse the two, for at night roles were, as it were, reversed. This, he informed me with an air of authority, was known as 'cruising', which was, apparently, not quite the same thing as 'trolling' and to be distinguished from 'looking for trade'. It appeared that Michael had learned (from where?) considerable codes of behaviour and rules of etiquette in detail that would have commanded the admiration of Lady Troubridge herself; and he gave me a lightning course in the proprieties and expected behaviour in gay encounters, in order that I might avoid misunderstanding, gaucherie and the strong possibility – which still remained – of being violently attacked if I mistook cues and promptings which it would take a lifetime to master.

In the wooded places, where the magenta tapers of willow-herb grew high and dense, a maze of paths had been cut. Men walked as though in a trance, apparently oblivious of those who were, nevertheless, their reason for being there. They pursued each other with the abstraction of contemplatives in a cloister; intense silence, as though in communion with no earthly powers. People would sit immobile for hours, bodies bronzed, hair bleached by the sun, tableaux of self-contained isolation in the clearings between the trees, where the grass was like burnt silk and seeds of thistledown drifted on the warm wind. It seemed sacrilegious to invade such spirituality.

Nights were different, peopled by noiseless shadows which flitted between the trees of which they appeared an emanation. Insubstantial figures looked fleetingly at each other, trying to discern features they did not want to see too clearly. Matches were struck; and in the crimson ogive of a protective hand, a flame trembled for a moment, lighting up a silhouette, a fall of hair, the colour of skin or eyes. These searchers in the dark had, it seemed, a great fear of trespassing, but whether upon fantasy or reality it was impossible to know.

Occasionally, they would write down your name in a notebook, adding it to a long list of first names and phone numbers. This, some said, was liberation. The point was to have fun, but to guard your heart against invasive emotion, so as not to get hurt. It seemed that Michael and I had been pioneers in heartlessness, except that our hearts had remained inviolate, unbroken by faithless lovers.

Many of the men I met made it clear they were not 'up for' a relationship. They had stopped their feelings at source, as though to stanch excessive bleeding from the wounds inflicted upon them. They had been hurt too many times. They had set free their feelings, only to find them abused and trampled on; they were not ready for a repeat of such pain. I marvelled that they had had the capacity to feel, yet to have rejected it. It must be a thing of small worth; and I told myself I was not missing much. I was surprised by the ease with which these men had repeatedly fallen in love, and how, from the experience of their 25 or 30 years, they had decided that a hardening of the heart was the principal prerequisite for survival.

ॐ ঙ্গ

Yet it was in this unpromising context that I met my lifelong companion. Actually, lifelong is something of an exaggeration: not only is life not yet finished, but I was already in my mid-thirties, so there was a strong sense that I met him in the nick of time, as it were, before I had settled for the annealed heart and recreational vacations in Thailand.

This development seemed to be also part of a scenario that had already been written. The symmetry of my life with Michael and Alastair, my departure, the reconstitution of our friendship and its ruin by the appearance of another stranger – although unexpected was completely unsurprising. The subjective consequences were disorienting and the influence it was to have upon the relationship between me and Michael was very disruptive. But there was a growing sense of exhaustion in our friendship; a feeling that, whatever consolations we had provided for each other, these were not going to be renewed in the depleted future we had contrived for ourselves in the spare décor of the flat. We were rarely alone, the telephone rang constantly and growing malnutrition from makeshift meals was masked by a pleasing euphoria created by a steady flow of alcohol.

I had entertained hopeless passions ever since I could remember, but they had existed in a separate sphere from my relationship with Michael. I ought to have challenged him. Perhaps our disbelief in emotional attachments applied only between us; but if that had been the case, why were we so drawn to each other? I wondered if Michael had ever experienced for others the same sentiments I harboured in vain? There was no sign that this was so. I certainly kept my own yearnings to myself, each one isolated, shaming and, as far I knew, unreciprocated; although when I mentioned, many years later, to an old school friend that I had harboured this carefully concealed desire for him, he said, 'Why ever didn't you tell me? I'm sure we could have done something about it'; and he spoke with such casual nonchalance that it took my breath away. While I had cowered in secrecy and silence over my infatuation, it had needed only a word or a smile, and the shame might simply have dissolved.

Or perhaps not. My mother's tormented relationship with her own sexuality, and with that of the men in her life, would inevitably affect her attitude to the unfolding maleness of me and my brother; a process which, given the disaster of her marriage to Sid and the refusal of Fred to have anything to do with his children, she would have prevented at all costs, had that been possible. As it was, every allusion to sex in my mother's conversation was surrounded with a sense of doom – shameful diseases, depths of misery, loneliness and abandonment were the unavoidable consequences: death, by contrast, was relatively cheerful. Even when we were small she issued premonitory warnings of which we could not possibly have had the slightest understanding. It was as though we were the bearers of some inherited disease (our gender!), which it was her duty to stifle or circumvent. She looked for signs of male incontinence even when we were infants: a blot of urine on our expensive underwear became an object of suspicion; and she timed our visits to the toilet with a precision that left no time for us to play with ourselves, if indeed, we had any inkling of the pleasures to be gained from such a (to us) implausible activity. We scarcely played with each other, let alone ourselves.

She and her siblings claimed to have grown up knowing nothing of what were grimly alluded to then as 'the facts of life'; although they were from a young age familiar with many of its fictions; which they duly transmitted to me and my brother, who treated them with a certain reserve, because, although we knew them to be false, we had no foundations on which to construct alternative truths.

If Michael denied my sexuality, this was familiar to me from the attempted erasure of it long practised by my mother. I yielded to it with something more than resignation: I was readily collusive with it, since this had long been a familiar experience. In any case, it seemed, it was my lot to provoke no excitement or interest in the breast of others; a certainty reinforced by the shameful and furtive minority to which I apparently belonged in that age of intolerance. In spite of this I spent much time looking into the face of every male pas-ser-by, wondering whether it registered the faintest interest in the unworthy and repellent person I imagined myself to be. Naturally, every such expedition confirmed everything I already thought I knew about myself.

So it was with no great expectation that I met my partner; and in the beginning he displayed no particular enthusiasm for my company or conversation; lingering only in the August twilight simply because he had nothing better to do.

But once established, the transformative power of the rela-tionship was a revelation. It was like being endowed with a faculty or a sense I had never known to exist; something like the gift of insight, which became as precious as vision itself; for it altered my perception of the world. Everything remained as it had been, but my view of things and people, and of their power shifted. Those who had appeared strong looked vulnerable, fallible; for the subjective change in the viewer also radically altered the response of the viewed to that altered gaze.

ℵ ℨ

It had never occurred to me that my feelings for anyone else could matter seriously to Michael; partly because he had assisted me so ably in extinguishing them. This was not the case, as soon became apparent when he thought he might lose, not only his ascendancy in the friendship but the friendship itself. I had compensated for his social dominance solely by being the principal actor and initiator of our writing together. He disliked my new acquaintance intensely; and went through a now-familiar process of disparagement and ridicule that grew in seriousness and intensity. I was surprised and scared by the vehemence of his dislike, and thought, perhaps, that his powers of penetration had perceived something that I, in my infatuation, had been unable to see. His knowledge of the world was, after all, so much more extensive than mine. I felt like a young Victorian woman in the presence of an authoritarian and sagacious father, who wished to preserve her from the attentions of a fortune-hunting adventurer; except that I had no fortune and, as had been frequently pointed out, no characteristics calculated to attach anyone to me for any conceivable ulterior motive. It was when Michael invoked our shared social class that I realised how seriously he took my defection. That my partner came from the suburbs of West London was offered up as the ultimately conclusive evidence of error. Michael actually said that I was betraying our families and parents by entering into a liaison with someone from suburbia; a place, the name of which he spoke with the contempt we normally reserved for the sites of wartime atrocity. To be accused of being a class traitor was as unique an experience as it was absurd; and I could scarcely believe what I heard.

That my own feelings could be awakened in the way I had experienced was frightening enough; to observe that Michael also had the capacity to be moved – and by one he had ostensibly merely tolerated out of a kind of charity – was even more disconcerting. There were, of course, other elements in the changing emotional scenery, but these were smothered by the immediacy of events. I had, after all, in my way, seduced Michael from his relationship with Alastair, promising a more congenial and creative way of living. Deserting him would come to appear a form of betrayal far different from the lurid defection from class solidarity that he had depicted. We had been competitive, secretive and unfaithful – part of the knot that had bound us together; and that was made clear only in the undoing of it. I was consumed by guilt, but not to the degree that I would renounce my independent relationship for the sake of the repressive bond that had, despite its limitations, served us well enough in the wintry season of blighted feelings.

There were wider revelations in this breaking of our friendship. It also provided some insight into how broader social and political changes occur: it is not that circumstances alter, but rather that what exists comes to be seen for what it is, or rather, for what it might well equally plausibly be. For instance, it would not take much of a shift to make all the big words deployed to keep us in our place appear as something else: democracy might suddenly come to appear as the management of organised impotence; freedom of choice a consolation for lost liberties; consumerism a caricature of prosperity. Political, like personal, power is always a delicate balance; and great efforts are required to maintain the illusion of the inevitability and immovability of things, because they are already in their 'natural' or already perfected state.

If Michael and I had not had such an awkward relationship with our selves – our sexual and emotional existence – we might have had an affectionate friendship, shorn, perhaps, of the very modest creativity our repressions engendered, but a direct, affirming solidarity in the light of our shared experience. As it was, we passed from childhood into each other's custody and vigilance; a kind of juvenile probation by unqualified personnel. This prolonged well into adult life dependency and denial we ought to have outgrown by late adolescence, since the society that had created these distortions in us had already changed, and presented an aspect of liberal tolerance a million miles away from the oppressive values that had dominated our early years. We were already in our mid-thirties when our relationship was disrupted from outside. It would never fully recover. Michael and I used to say to people that 'we failed to grow up together'. Intended as a lightly amusing *bon mot*, it turned out to be an accurate assessment of the way we had inhibited one another's independence.

All of this I thought about only later. My partner moved into the flat with Michael and me; and a strange symmetrical similarity with our earlier *ménage à trois* was established. This was equally fragile and destined to a quick end. We moved out; my partner and I bought a house in what had once been the salubrious suburb of West Norwood, not far from the balmy airs of the Crystal Palace and Beulah Spa. Michael remained, to turn the flat into an even more ornate monument to his liberation, a kind of Victor Emmanuel structure celebrating the supremacy of sexuality. If I felt guilty, this was allayed by Michael's apparent indifference to my departure. I assumed his absence of any display of feeling indicated his victory over such weaknesses, a victory, which, despite intensive tutelage and willingness to learn on my part, I had never quite achieved. In this, as in so much else, I was also mistaken.

ഇ   ൠ

When Janet could no longer live on her own, she moved into the dreadfully named British Home and Hospital for Incurables in Streatham. (It was known by its initials, BHHI, and Janet referred to it, rather benignly, as the Beehive). An imposing structure, it had been established in the 1870s for 'the middle classes who had formerly lived in comfort and respectability, and who had been reduced by incurable diseases to the most distressing poverty. For these the institution provided the best medical attendance, good nursing and all the comforts of a home.' Not admitted were patients of 'the insane, idiotic and pauper classes'.

By the late twentieth century the extreme pietism of its founders had abated somewhat, but still lingered: it threaded its way along the polished banisters, insinuated itself in spaces beyond ornamental cupolas and lurked in starched sheets and unappetising food. The building was a monument to self-conscious philanthropy. A carved tympanum over the main entrance represented a Samaritan dragging a corpse-like figure towards some kind of hospice, but wind and rain had effaced much of the detail. A plaque declared, 'Times change and we must change with them,' an observation perhaps those in the last stages of illness might more charitably have been spared. It was in this cool monumental shelter that Janet would spend the last years of her life.

In the corridor on the ground floor stood a granite obelisk, endowed by Prince Christian of Schleswig-Holstein in July 1882.* A quotation from Gregory of Nazianzen, with whose work in the fourth century on the nature of the Trinity most

---

* Prince Christian was a Danish-born German prince who became a member of the British royal family on his marriage to Princess Helena, fifth child of Queen Victoria and Prince Albert.

of the residents were doubtless familiar, stated, 'Sorrow is not immortal. Let us not aggravate our griefs with ungenerous thoughts. If we have been bereaved of blessings, we have enjoyed them too. To be bereft is the lot of all; to enjoy is not the lot of many.' Such was the nature of the consolations provided by this institution. Many doubtless derived great comfort from them. Janet did not.

At the Beehive Janet befriended many members of staff, not only because they came from all over the world, and had tales to tell of epic dispossession and loss, but also because she depended upon their goodwill to be turned in bed during the night, to make phone calls for her and to turn the pages of her book. She taught English to a Somali woman and a Tamil from Sri Lanka. She retained her capacity for attentive listening, and absorbed with undiminished indignation stories of torture, discrimination and flight from violent regimes.

Since the house I shared with my partner was less than a mile from the institution, I frequently visited Janet on Sunday afternoons, the most dismal time of the week. Tremulous hymn-singing came from the cavernous chapel. The chaplain's well-meaning words of consolation, Janet said, took unfair advantage of his spiritual captives. These were in no position to question promises of a better life hereafter, since nothing could be worse than their present condition. If Janet concealed her unbelief from her parents, this was because she could not bear to wound them with such knowledge. Both outlived her and went through one of the greatest of tragedies, which is that of a child dying before her parents. Her father officiated at her funeral.

On summer afternoons I would wheel her chair into the garden, where a bed of Mme Pierre Auger roses gave off a scent even more intoxicating than the Chanel Numéro Cinq with which Janet tried to cover the whiff of mortality that pervaded the building. She closed her eyes against the sunshine, as its warmth burnt off the chill of enforced sanctity from her flesh. By this stage, she wore a scarf around her forehead, tied to the head-rest of the chair, since she had lost control of the neck-muscles. As the sclerosis (not called multiple, for nothing, she observed) took away not only her voluntary movements, but impaired her reflexes also. Janet said she had little to do but listen to the progression of the illness within, wondering what humiliation it would next visit upon her. Would she lose sight, hearing, memory, control of her bowels, swallowing or breathing?

Janet had always loved to memorise poetry: Baudelaire, Cavafy, Marvell, Lorca; a facility which proved a blessing as her eyesight began to fail and she was driven back onto her plentiful inner resources. As her vision weakened, we printed out new poems in large type, which we placed on a lectern close to her chair. She turned the pages with the help of a small rubber-tipped spatula operated by mouth. She raced to commit to memory poems that would survive the descent into darkness. In particular she loved Dante.

Al poco giorno ed al gran cerchio d'ombra
Son giunto, lasso! al bianchir dei colli
Quando si perde lo color nell'erba.
Ed il moi disio non cangia il verde
Si e barbato nella pietra dura
Che parla e sente come fosse donna*

Her photograph was published in one of the Home's fund-raising posters. Sitting in a wheelchair, she is clearly reading Nadezhda Mandelstam's *Hope Against Hope*; a message which surely passed by the administrators of the charity. Janet said that few people understood that those with degenerative

---

* 'I have come, alas, to the time of short daylight and the great circle of shadow, which whitens the hills and drains all colour from the grass. But my desire is still green, held fast, as it is, in the hardest stone, that speaks and feels as though it were woman.'

diseases needed, above all, to express rage at what was happening to them. 'Most visitors think they have to be resolutely bright and cheerful. You experience this as violence, because it is a denial of you, as though we could be distracted from our fate by *their* ability to bear our suffering.'

Some Sundays Janet would visit us; occasionally we booked an ambulance, but when it was fine we wheeled her through the streets. Many of her friends came to sit in our garden, where she drank dry Martini through a straw and ate strawberries and cream. After sunset, we would wheel her back, as people were returning from their Sunday afternoon excursions. They would stand aside for us to pass, smiling, and perhaps thanking God that they and their families had been spared such visitations. Once returned to the crepuscular atmosphere of the Beehive, we sometimes helped her undress, since other residents had already long been in bed. We kissed her goodnight before passing over her care to a competent but, of course, over-stretched, staff.

One Friday morning the nursing sister called. Janet was asking to see me. I should come as quickly as possible, since she was very ill. She was lying in bed, her breathing shallow. The sunlight struggled with the breeze in the pale curtains. Her niece from Norway was there, and I said I would come back the following day.

I walked in the July sunshine, intensely conscious of the beauty and fragility of life. Geraniums blazed in the hanging baskets, and petunias trumpeted their vivid blue notes against the brick. Next morning I reached the hospital at about ten thirty. Her bed was empty. 'I've come to see Janet.' 'Are you her brother?' 'No, I am her friend.' 'I'm afraid she died in the night.'

I was asked if I wanted to see her. I don't know why I said no. I have never been afraid of the dead, especially of those I have loved. Perhaps it was because of the strange unexpectedness of the inevitable.

Neither did I attend her funeral. Every time I had seen her in the recent past had been a moment of grief for some aspect of loss in her long decline. I already knew the meaning of mourning in advance. I was to go to India for work. When I reached Mumbai a few days later, I thought I would perform a slightly extravagant private ceremony of which Janet would approve. I bought an armful of red roses, and went to Nariman Point, where the Parsee widows in their billowing white dresses promenaded sedately in the humid monsoon breeze. I threw the flowers, one by one onto the rocks of the polluted Arabian Sea, where the crimson buds were soon lost in the foam.

    ℬ   ℛ

When I left the flat for what Michael called contemptuously, 'bourgeois domesticity', he turned the apartment into an even more florid temple, so that it came to resemble a medieval torture chamber. In this setting Michael could express more fully the fierce ambiguities of his attachments. For some months he lived with a Frenchman, whose desire to be hurt far exceeded Michael's capacity to inflict pain: his speciality had always been confined to the psychological. Michael later told me that after Hervé had left, he found a cupboard full of the blood-stained dressings he had used for wounds he had received from those less squeamish than Michael.

The loss of Michael was like a bereavement; and I have often wondered at the readiness with which we break up or separate from those we loved or thought we loved; since this is only to mimic death, which takes us all away from one another at last. Perhaps it is the sense of power that derives from the dispensability of a worn-out relationship; and while the history of people – especially women – compelled to live with those who oppress them is long enough not to wish involuntary permanence on anyone – it seems that many of our deepest relationships have been balefully affected by a throwaway culture, which has disposed of waste without, until very recently, concern for the pollutants it engenders. Something similar is perhaps true of the less tangible waste products of galloping emotional consumption.

This is not to say that my rupture with Michael was not long overdue; but it came at a high cost. It would not have happened, if it had not been for a more direct and fulfilling relationship of a kind that had been made impossible between me and Michael; partly because of the circumstances in which we had met, the culture in which we had grown, the abrasive nature of our temperament and the competitiveness we professed to abhor, but which animated much of our life together.

The breaking of our dependency in the long run freed us both. It was the relationship – created in adversity and fear for our mutual protection – that was at fault. For within two or three years Michael also met someone who transformed his life. He was more than fifteen years younger than Michael; and once his new relationship was established, a kind of reconciliation became possible. Michael's partner had a sweetness which sometimes masked his acuity and intelligence. They met one New Year's Eve in an almost-deserted gay bar; and it did not take long before Michael dismantled his altar to sexuality, moved out of the flat, which by that time had become dingy, the ceiling stained with damp, the flimsy furniture barely standing. He and his partner moved into the first home Michael had ever really made independently. We had enough in common to make a friendly social relationship, although it was always rather fragile, and coloured by the history between me and Michael; and while much of that evaporated with time, it left a stain which never disappeared completely. Michael used to say his partner would look after him when he grew old; although this was not to be, since he died of a brain haemorrhage in his mid-fifties.

This was a severe blow to Michael who, at almost the same time, developed bowel cancer. His own ill health was so overwhelming that he was not able to mourn the death of his partner adequately. During this time, we met frequently, and something of the old familiarity was re-established. We even started to write again, although by this time the moment for what we had regarded as our anarchic wit had passed; or perhaps our capacity to amuse had been muted by experience.

Two strokes followed Michael's recovery from cancer. Inevitably, this changed him. He became more irritable, because more frustrated. He had difficulty walking. It also made him revert to a resentment towards me and my partner. He felt the injustice of the death of his own life companion and his own ill health, while my partner and I remained – temporarily – relatively unscathed by time. He rejected what he saw as being patronised; but at the same time became heavily dependent on the woman who became his principal carer. Although engaged for specific purposes, she dealt with his administration of the house, his housework, his money, and his comfort and cleanliness. She came to love him dearly, and of all those who grieved when he died, hers was the most genuine.

Sometimes we went with Michael to the theatre or cinema. Even when he could barely walk, he refused to take my arm, but would sometimes permit my partner to guide him down steps or on slippery surfaces. We would take him to a place where a taxi could be easily hailed. He would get into the vehicle, and once we had parted, he never looked back or waved or acknowledged us in any way.

The death of his partner had left him very well off. He went on cruises, some of which were very expensive; and he paid for relative strangers to accompany him. Some of these were pleased to offer the company and support on a trip to Papua New Guinea and to the Solomon Islands, which had been an area of study of Michael's anthropology degree. Others saw an open financial opportunity, and sometimes asked him for significant sums of money. He was protected by his carer against the most predatory. I sometimes said to him that he did not recognise who his true friends were; and he gave me to understand that whoever they were, I was certainly not among them.

It was after his third stroke and an extended stay in hospital that he was transferred to the nursing home at Norwood Junction; a quiet retreat behind a decayed High Street, where nail bars, Turkish men's hairdressers, betting shops and payday loans had become the principal amenities.

I visited him regularly in the three months he lived. I always took him a box of raspberries, his favourite fruit. He was said by the staff to be 'cantankerous'. He was sometimes abusive, but by this time his mind had become clouded, his memory uncertain. I did not see him in the three weeks before his death, because another friend had died in the middle of that December. On Boxing Day morning, a call came from a former colleague of Michael's that he was dying. We should go at once if we wanted to see him.

By the time we had driven to South London, it was too late.

❧ ❧

At the funeral I delivered a eulogy; but it was a poor apology for all the things we never said to each other.

What might I have said to Michael before he died? 'You always promised adventure and romance in some way. You had the gift of spontaneity. You would say, "Come on, let's go somewhere." One Easter Monday, when we were about fifteen, we went to Woburn Abbey. It was a beautiful day. I can remember the cirrus-scratched blue of the sky and how the warm wind stirred waves of daffodils in the park. The excitement of having no transport home was, to me, very daring and frightening. It was a golden day. At about the same time, we went to stay with your Auntie Doll in London. I was utterly at your mercy. It was the first time I had ever seen the panic of the rush hour, the first time on a London bus. It travelled miles up the Seven Sisters Road, out through Southgate into Enfield. You were perfectly competent and always knew where we were. I was very dependent. I gave your auntie some lavish present in gratitude for a sleepless night in cold sheets under an open window.'

I have another memory, a fusion of hundreds of times we were together. We were always walking about, somewhat incongruously, because I was very tall and I stooped so that I did not present too great a contrast with Michael, who was of middle height. We walked over the fields on warm evenings when we were in the sixth form. We would imagine the fate of the last inhabitants of abandoned cottages, only the foundations and outlines of hovels filled with brambles, ivy and wild flowers. Did they die of the plague, the last inhabitant left with no one in earshot as she choked on the last crumbs of wheaten loaf? Did the local landowner evict the residents in order to create parkland which, once the site was empty, he could not afford to complete? Were the people simply dispersed, going into service or emigrating to bigger villages for employment? We filled the vacant spaces with our historic fantasies, excited and scared by the hallucinatory power of our joint imaginings. There was something eerie and evocative in the cawing of the rooks in the elm trees and the wind in the rank grass; and we would imagine a similar fate overtaking bigger towns in the event of nuclear war which was, at that time, always present. Together, we read John Hersey's *Hiroshima*, repelled and fascinated by his accounts of people transfigured into living skeletons, skin covered with the pattern of a burnt kimono, the spontaneous combustion of greenery in the parks to which survivors had fled for safety. Our adolescent minds were haunted by the thought of annihilation, which appeared to us a real possibility, the more terrifying because we had so much to accomplish in our lives.

We walked everywhere. Reluctant to go home after our evenings spent in social exploration, we would visit the only cafe in the town that stayed open until ten o'clock, or walk round the park, through its sedate municipal layout, where a crumbling bandstand no longer reverberated with Sousa marches and exotic birds had ceased to moult in their wire cages, refusing to show the blue-and-green fan of their feathers, sulking with their golden head beneath their wing, as out of place in this miserable zoo as we felt we were. We walked past the 'Fever Hospital', where people still held their breath as they passed by for fear of catching something. We lingered in the cemetery where we tried to imagine the lives of inconsolable relicts and small children carried away by diphtheria or scarlet fever. We knew every street in the town, especially those where remaining slum properties brought to life the stories of evictions, moonlit flits, bailiffs, and belongings piled on a handcart; stories we had collected from a dying generation of leather-workers, just as they had collected pressed flowers in family Bibles or a case of butterflies impaled on pins on the parlour wall. We walked home after the cinema, still laughing over *Cat Women of the Moon*, which had been so poorly edited that we had caught sight of an object labelled The Million-Dollar Bubble Machine. We watched the emptying of the town centre, where a functionary blew a whistle at 10.30 to announce the departure of the last buses, so that no one should have any excuse to be late for work in the morning.

Wherever we went, we always took a longer way round than was necessary, because we were always unwilling to separate.

I felt that Michael possessed something I needed, and he was always full of entertainment, improvisation, drama. If we prolonged the time spent together, this was because we knew that no one else's company could equal the pleasure we found in each other's.

We took day trips to London, where, on Saturdays, it was possible to visit three theatres in a single day, a matinee at 2.30, another at 5.0 and an evening performance at 8.0. One day we saw *The Punch Revue*, T.S. Eliot's *The Confidential Clerk* and, I think, Sandy Wilson's *The Boy Friend*, rushing from one theatre to the next before the curtain had fallen in order not to miss the following performance. We scarcely knew what we had seen, and I have virtually no memory of these spectacles; that we had been to the theatre three times in a single day was enough.

Later, at weekends we sometimes went from Cambridge to stay in Sue's flat in Paddington with her and friends from the Central School of Speech and Drama. Sue had been a member of our dramatic society in Northampton, and she made a career as actor. The flat was in Paddington, unbelievably grimy, squalid and enchanting. We slept five in a bed, and kept our clothes on, because the sheets were black with dirt and the stains of the sticky jam sandwiches we ate for our impoverished supper. Sue went to Canada, and with her husband founded a theatre in a mid-west city, which had remained a stranger to the finer things in life. She said it reminded her of our efforts to bring culture to Northampton. She fell ill while performing as Lady Macbeth; was diagnosed with cancer and died within a fortnight. She spent the time with preparatory administration of her own death, making arrangements for her two small children. She was thirty-eight. A few months later, I went to visit her mother in Northampton. It was a mild January day. I took a bunch of snowdrops. She looked at me sadly, and her thoughts were so plain – 'Why could it not have been you, who have no attachments, who died, rather than my lovely daughter' – that I made some excuse and left.

80 CR

Michael and I were also early enthusiasts of vox pop interviews. On the occasion of the wedding of Princess Margaret, we thought we would like to talk to the people who had spent the night in the Mall, in order to get a better view of the procession, because we wanted to learn something about the nature of people whose affection for the royal family was so intense they would endure such discomfort simply for a fleeting view of the couple. We went to our respective tutors to ask for an *exeat*, since students were forbidden to be absent from Cambridge for a certain number of nights in the term, and a residential qualification was also a necessary preamble to taking a degree. When asked why we wanted the *exeat*, we said it was to attend the wedding. Both tutors assumed that we were to be guests at the ceremony – no doubt many other undergraduates had taken a couple of days off for that very reason. We found it hard to contain our amusement. We spent the night talking to people who had come from all over the country for the royal event. We wrote up our 'findings', but made no attempt to publish them. The outing was its own reward.

Everything we did together was diverting, unpredictable and funny. I feel so sad, Michael, that we never managed to say how much we cared for each other, and failed to examine what bitter-sweet compulsions bound us together. We later came to recognise and to regret the arrogance and absurdity of our contrived picaresque journey; we were able to see as pitiable our pretentiousness and false sense of superiority, and, in the light of grief, loss and disillusionment, acknowledged that our posturing was far from the originality we thought we represented; was, in fact, simply an aspect of the delayed maturing of young people at a time when youth was becoming one of the most highly prized and lucrative commodities of the Western world.

But we never spoke of our mutual affection, attachment or companionability; although all were present, if suppressed, in an apparently impersonal relationship. Animated by a desire to appear smart and invulnerable, dissimulating all emotion, instead of expressing what we might have felt had we had access to, that – to us – most mysterious and unfathomably dangerous realm of experience, our feelings, which remained like bats in daylight, clustered securely away from the light and air. We thought it our life's purpose to be clever, when simply being together ought to have been more than enough. We were never slow to profess solidarity with workers, the poor and the oppressed of the world; but we were unable to express it where it mattered most – to each other.

The pictures of Michael and me standing were taken at the time of Peter Gill's production of *Life Price* at the Royal Court in 1969 – they were, I think, taken by the *Daily Mail* for an interview. On the following pages, the poster is for a play at the Theatre Upstairs at the Royal Court which ran in July–August 1975. The picture of Janet is from the garden in West Norwood where I lived with my partner. The picture of Michael and me outside Kudos Gay Bar was taken in the 1990s. The last one of me and Michael is in the gardens of our flat in Dorchester Court, Herne Hill, in the early 1970s.

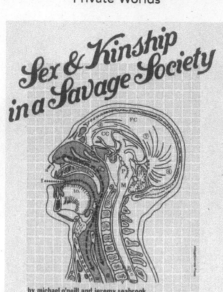

by michael o'neill and jeremy seabrook.
directed by william alexander, designed by david short,
with tom bell, lynn farleigh, lucita lijertwood,
doreen mantle and robert putt.
at the theatre upstairs, royal court theatre,
sloane square sw1, 01-730 2554. 24 july to 16 august.

THE THEATRE UPSTAIRS

Thanks to our Patreon subscriber:

Ciaran Kane

Who has shown generosity and comradeship in support of our publishing.

Check out the other perks you get by subscribing to our Patreon – visit patreon.com/plutopress.

Subscriptions start from £3 a month.